CUTCH
OR
RANDOM SKETCHES

DURRANI HORSEMAN,

in the service and pay of the Rao of Cutch.

CUTCH
OR
RANDOM SKETCHES,
TAKEN DURING A RESIDENCE IN ONE OF THE NORTHERN PROVINCES OF

WESTERN INDIA;
INTERSPERSED WITH
LEGENDS AND TRADITIONS.

BY MRS. POSTANS

ILLUSTRATED WITH ENGRAVINGS FROM ORIGINAL DRAWINGS BY THE AUTHOR.

GYAN

Published by

GYAN

Gyan Publishing House
5, Ansari Road
Daryaganj, New Delhi-110002
Phone: 011-47034999, 9811692060
E-mail: books@gyanbooks.com

Distribution Network
gyanbooks.com
India, USA, Canada, UK, Australia, France

ISBN : 978-81-212-3287-6 (PB)
First Published, 1839

2nd Impression 2020

Printed at: Gyan Press, Delhi.

Cutch or Random Sketches
Author: Mrs. Postans

CUTCH;

OR,

RANDOM SKETCHES,

TAKEN DURING A RESIDENCE IN ONE OF
THE NORTHERN PROVINCES OF

WESTERN INDIA;

INTERSPERSED WITH

Legends and Traditions.

BY MRS. POSTANS.

ILLUSTRATED WITH ENGRAVINGS FROM ORIGINAL DRAWINGS
BY THE AUTHOR.

LONDON:
SMITH, ELDER AND CO. CORNHILL.

1839.

Front Projection of Doorway of Rao Lackas' Tomb.

TO

THE RIGHT HONOURABLE

JOHN FITZGIBBON,

EARL OF CLARE,

LATE GOVERNOR OF BOMBAY,

&c. &c. &c.

MY LORD,

The honour your Lordship has conferred on me, by allowing your name to be prefixed to this unpretending volume, is highly flattering.

For such a favour I should not have presumed to hope, had I not been aware of your Lordship's liberality of sentiment; the subject also being one with which your Lordship is well acquainted, and in which you have taken considerable interest.

In this, my first attempt to place myself

before the public in the responsible position of an author, many errors may probably be discovered, for which I feel convinced your Lordship will be disposed to entertain every generous indulgence.

In the anxious hope, therefore, that, should the ensuing pages be found deficient in actual importance, they may offer something for the amusement of a few leisure hours,

I have the honour to subscribe myself,

With the highest respect,

My Lord,

Your Lordship's most grateful,

Most obedient,

Very humble Servant,

MARIANNE POSTANS.

INTRODUCTION.

Some time resident in the province of Cutch, and remarking with much interest many local peculiarities, I am led to imagine that a few slight sketches of its more striking characteristics may be thought worthy of notice.

General acquaintance with the remote stations which form a considerable part of our Indian possessions is very limited; and as Cutch, from its geographical position, as well as from its maritime importance, is likely to become connected with the favourite and apparently feasible plan of steam-navigation on the Indus, it will perhaps be deemed more deserving of attention than other stations not likely to be in any way affected by the progress of commercial civilization.

As European society in the East has been frequently and admirably described, and as military camps in India differ little except in size, I have restricted myself to the attempt of delineating the characteristics of the country, and of the various tribes which compose its native population.

In noticing the natural productions of Cutch, I have not ventured to offer any description in scientific terms. Throughout the work, I have frequently diverged from the immediate subject, to offer such reflections as were suggested by the occasion, and which I trust will not be regarded as impertinent by the reader.

These pages are the result of a series of notes, taken during a residence of some years in Cutch; during which I have enjoyed unusual opportunities of becoming acquainted with the general and domestic manners of the population in its various castes.

The illustrative engravings are all from original designs, which, as productions of an amateur artist, will, I hope, equally with the literary sketches, be honoured with the indulgent suffrage of the reader.

CAMP, BHOOJ:
Sept. 29th, 1837.

CONTENTS.

CHAPTER IV.

THE HAREM.

CHAPTER V.

HINDU TOMBS.

CHAPTER VI.

SUTTEE.

CHAPTER VII.

ANJAR.

CHAPTER VIII.

THE RUNN.

CHAPTER IX.

RELIGIOUS CEREMONIES IN CUTCH.

THE NAGA PACHAMI.

CHAPTER X.

RELIGIOUS SECTS IN CUTCH.

CHAPTER XI.

THE MILITARY TRIBES OF CUTCH.

CHAPTER XII.

CASTLES IN CUTCH.

CHAPTER XIII.

INFANTICIDE IN CUTCH.

CHAPTER XIV.

RUINS IN CUTCH.

CHAPTER XV.

PILGRIMS.

CHAPTER XVI.

WORKMEN OF CUTCH.

CHAPTER XVII.

MINSTRELSY OF CUTCH.

CHAPTER XVIII.

ON THE BARDS AND BARDIC LITERATURE OF CUTCH.

CHAPTER XIX.

ON THE ART OF DESIGN, AND THE GENERAL WANT OF INSTRUCTION IN CUTCH.

CHAPTER XX.

JUGGLING, SNAKE-CHARMING, AND MAGIC.

CHAPTER XXI.

PRODUCTIONS OF CUTCH.

CHAPTER XXII.

CONCLUSION.

GENERAL VIEW OF CUTCH.

LIST OF EMBELLISHMENTS.

GEOGRAPHICAL POSITION

OF THE

PROVINCE OF CUTCH.

CUTCH is situated in the most northern part of Western India, within the 68th and 70th degrees of east longitude; and the 22d and 24th parallels of north latitude.

It is bounded on the west, by the river Indus; on the east by the Gulf of Cutch, and the salt desert of the Runn; on the north, by the Great Desert; and on the south, by the sea. The province is about one hundred and sixty miles in length, from east to west; and sixty-five in breadth, from north to south; and is distant about five hundred miles from the Presidency of Bombay.

RANDOM SKETCHES,

&c. &c.

CHAPTER I.

THE VOYAGE.

Embarkation. — Scenery of Bombay. — Steam Vessels. — Departure. — Colabah Light-House. — Description of a Cutch Kotia, or Native Boat.—Indolence and Filthiness of the Crew.—Arrival at Mandavie.

It was early in the month of January, that, under promise of a fair and freshening breeze, we embarked on board a Cutch Kotia, and left our anchorage in the Harbour of Bombay.

The morning was bright and beautiful; the sun, just risen, had shed his early radiance on the wooded summits of Elephanta; the fishermen were returning with their spoils; the merry capstan songs resounded from the decks of the English merchantmen; and, far as the eye could gaze, it rested on a scene teeming with interest and animation. The time was favourable, and we observed these picturesque effects, as adding much to the usual beauty of the view; for although the natural loveliness of the island-skirted harbour of Bombay has been rendered familiar to the imagination, by the pen and pencil of the most accomplished masters, its peculiar interest depends much on what an artist would call accident; such as the brightness of the lights, the softness of the shadows, and the variety, number, and picturesque character of the native boats, which, by the aid of their well filled latteen sails, skim like sea-birds on the surface of the deep. As these various craft round the richly wooded headlands, and make towards the harbour, crossing, recrossing, and chasing each other, few scenes can present so much interest and beauty, enlivened as it is by the bright sunshine of a tropical climate, and the joyous shouts which re-echo from numerous fishing boats, as their laughing crews outstrip the heavier vessels.

An additional interest is now given to the harbour of Bombay by the presence of the fine steam-packets which have lately been appointed to advance the interests dependent on an overland communication. True, they add little to its picturesque effect, but they do far more: they afford a promise of civilization to the shores of India, such as no other means could compass; and, to the minds of her English sojourners, a hope which makes the exile's "heart sing for joy."

Few persons can leave Bombay without regret. Its lovely scenery, its hospitable society, and its civilized condition cannot but charm the English visitor; and when duty commands that he should resign its pleasures, the voyager does so with a sigh, and as his boat recedes from the shore, and the gay tents on the esplanade dwindle to mere specks, full many a wistful glance does he cast back to that distant scene of life and enjoyment.

The last object which appears in sight to interest the voyager is the light-house on Colabah; that past, he finds his little craft tossing about in a heavy sea, and is speedily overwhelmed with the miseries that surround him. At this point adverse winds frequently spring up; the boat, long out of sight of land, pitches and rolls, and is yet unable to make way; the servants, suffering and useless, lie rolled up in their blankets upon the deck; the spray extinguishes the fire; and the poor, sick, weather-wearied voyager would willingly, like Gonzalo, "give a thousand furlongs of sea for an acre of barren ground, long heath, brown furze, any thing," so intolerable has his state become.

In a few days, however, matters improve; a favourable breeze carries him within sight of the opposite coast, and the Portuguese cook, who is always the earliest convalescent, pops up his black head, and commences culinary preparations.

A dogged state of patient endurance succeeds one of actual suffering; and, although the long sandy line of coast which lies under his view can present nothing to attract the interest of the voyager, a calm sea and a favourable breeze tend materially to restore both his appetite and his tranquillity.

Much has been said against sea-voyaging; keenly have its miseries been felt, and as severely, perhaps, anathematized.

The perfect accommodation provided by the English merchantmen relieves the Eastern passenger from many of its horrors, providing him with resources and comforts of no common order; but on arriving in India, he finds his miseries commence.

The majority of the northern nations under the Bombay presidency are so situated, that a residence in any of the states involves the necessity of a tedious and wearying voyage; and the poor Anglo-Indian, whose duty attaches him to some *up*-station, (as it is called,) several hundred miles, perhaps, from Bombay, too soon discovers, that a boat is the only conveyance adapted to his means and position. And with that bitter feeling of unadaptation to circumstances, which a constrained traveller ever feels so keenly, in a country of primitive habits, he suddenly finds himself, his servants, and all his worldly possessions on board a native cotton-boat, the appearance of which is equally dirty, awkward, and unsafe.

The boat in which we embarked for Cutch was of the rudest construction, half decked, and totally deficient in privacy, accommodation, and cleanliness. It has been my fate to be a frequent voyager in native boats, which are always dirty and inconvenient, but I have never seen any so rife with offence as a Cutch Kotia. These boats, from their peculiar build, roll and pitch dreadfully; they boast but one cabin, which is divided horizontally, and, from the ridiculous lowness of both its compartments, seems to have been intended only for the accommodation of an upper and a lower stratum of monkeys: moreover, so infested are they with rats, and every other description of the most uncompanionable vermin, that the sensitive voyager must either occupy the hold in joint tenure with his horses, dogs, and luggage, or devote himself to a full endurance of their attacks in the little den courteously yclept a cabin, the single door of which gives full admission to the unsavoury steams of ghee, onions, and dried fish, which are at all times under culinary preparation. The crew of these boats are usually half Hindu, and half Mahomedan; they are a satisfied and slothful race, who lie scattered about the poop, or on the rafters of the bows during the noontide heat, with the exception of the helmsman, alternately sleeping and smoking until sunset, when they assemble round a large platter of rice, curry, and coarse grain cakes, which, after the prefatory measure of pouring a little water over their hands, they rapidly despatch — sitting round in a circle, and gathering up the rice between their fingers, each dipping into the same dish.

I have never on any occasion observed the crew use water for the purposes of ablution; neither have I seen any attempt made to cleanse a boat, or to put it into any sort of order. The whole scene is one of filth and confusion; fowl coops, cocoa-nuts, cooking vessels, coir ropes and passengers mingled together, and surrounded by every ill savour that bilge-water and native cookery can produce.

A boat's crew can imagine no state of existence half so desirable as one of rest; they consequently display a total apathy as to their amount of daily progress. If a foul wind set in, they immediately anchor; and if at night a fair breeze should spring up, they never set sail again, but remain very quietly until the following morning: thus they can have no sympathy with their unhappy passenger, whose every sense furnishes him with fresh avenues for disgust and suffering. Remonstrance is vain; but daily does he groan in spirit, as the approach of evening sees him little advanced on his weary way, and the crew again prepare, even under a fair wind, and a refreshing breeze, to drop anchor, and wait the morning tide.

To enlarge on the miseries of such a locale is needless; many of my readers may have experienced them, and memory will readily complete the sketch.

During the rainy season, which occupies four months of the year, all water communication ceases between the province of Cutch and Bombay: the post-bag, fortunately, makes its way over a tedious, and very circuitous overland route, but even this advantage is rendered very precarious from the badness of the roads, and the swollen state of the hill torrents.

During the winter months the voyage to Cutch frequently occupies from ten to twenty days, but in very favourable seasons it may be made in four.

The Cutch boats are fortunately very strong in their construction, and their Tindals * are well acquainted with the route; accidents are rare, and foul weather is seldom experienced. In the event of a squall coming on, the crew immediately run into some of the numerous creeks along the shore, and anchor for fair weather;—a tedious, yet satisfactory measure, as the crew, being

* Captains.

all fatalists, are little inclined to make any exertion in the hour of danger, and commonly content themselves with counting their beads, and calling on their respective Gods; rather, however, as it seems, from an impulse of physical fear, than from any hope of being succoured by providential aid.

After leaving the light-house of Bombay, the Cutch boats, as I have already described, stretch out to sea, and near the opposite coast of Kattiwar, which is flat and sandy in its character; and if I except the fortified town of Pore-Brender, and the celebrated Hindoo temple at D'waka, which I shall have occasion to mention elsewhere, this long line of coast is a mere burning solitude, undiversified by any object calculated to excite the voyager's interest.

In sight of this dreary prospect the boat remains for days, tacking and anchoring, as calms or foul winds may require; until, after crossing the Gulf of Cutch, the white bastions of a walled town appear, and the little craft anchors safely, in the roadstead of Mandavie.

CHAPTER II.

MANDAVIE.

Harbour.—Population.—Etymology of the word "Cutch."—Commerce. —Boat-building.—Pilots.—Arab Sailors.—Characteristics of Mandavie, and of its Inhabitants.—Palace.—Story of Ram Sing, the Architect.—Agriculture.—Female Costume.—Holidays.—Climate. —Fish. — Ruins of the City of Raipoor. — Legend of Vere and Vicramaditya, Grandsons of Indra.—Illustration.—The Nine Gems of the Court of Vicramaditya.—Road to Bhooj.—Cutch Carts.— Town of Kaira. — Manufacture of Cotton Cloths. — Mahomedan Temple.—Women of Kaira.

On approaching the Province of Cutch,* the coast affords few attractions to the traveller's eye, presenting as it does, a mere sandy outline, slightly diversified by a few patches of stunted vegetation,

* Probably so called from "Cach" or Cach'ha, signifying a low maritime country. In the prophetic chapters of the Puránás, two brothers are mentioned as Puru-Cach'ha and Buja-Cach'ha. One of these, tradition asserts to have been the founder of the ancient city of Teja, in Cach, a country whose geographical position agrees with the present province of Cutch. "When the Greeks sailed within sight of land," says the

and straggling palm trees; but on landing at Mandavie, which is the principal sea-port, an appearance of wealth and unusual bustle excites the traveller's attention. A creek, which runs skirting one side of the city for about a mile inland, has its mouth filled with boats, making, mending, receiving, or discharging cargo; whilst carts of a peculiarly rude construction drawn by strong and sturdy bullocks, struggle through the heavy sand laden with goods for the interior.

The inhabitants seem a busy, cheerful, and industrious race, and their peculiarly bright and varied costume gives an appearance of gaiety to the place, which is strikingly pleasing, and seldom seen in an Indian town of second rate importance. The population is principally composed of Banyans, Brahmins, and cultivators; many of whom may be seen on the outside of the town, either engaged in their several callings, loitering lazily

learned Essayist on the era of Vicramaditya, "they coasted along the Delta, as far as the point of land before mentioned (Jakow,) and then crossed the Gulf of Cach'ha, thus called from a famous town of that name, still existing. This headland is particularly noticed by the author of the Periplus (Arrian). The mussulmans, bolder, crossed from the western mouth of the Indus to an island called Avicama, a district near D'waka." Abul Fazel in 1582, describes the province as barren and unproductive; the interior almost unknown, but the situation of its seaports similar to those at present described.

along, or grouped together in little knots, gossipping with vehement gesticulation, on any trifling subject, of profit or pleasure. Here and there, a retainer of the Rao* comes swaggering along, displaying the superior height, aquiline nose, and long moustache of the Rajpoot tribe; his arms are a sword, shield, and matchlock, and his dress and bearing are marked by an air of mingled haughtiness, foppery, and independence. Then are seen swarthy but fine-limbed children, rolling on the soft sand in childish glee, and shouting with joy, as a horseman passes them, circling and passaging with consummate skill, his gaily decorated steed. Near these, a water-carrier urges on his bullock, which, laden with the water bags, slowly saunters forward, whilst his master smokes his hookah, and indulges in a passing chat with the women, who, gracefully bearing their earthen water-vessels on their heads, are returning to the well to which he journeys. Lastly, are groups of women, employed in sifting grain from light baskets, in which they display the most graceful attitudes; the passing breeze winnows the corn, as it falls into large heaps, and numerous asses wait leisurely around, to carry it in sacks to the merchants' granaries.

The creek which I have alluded to, runs up from the sea, near the usual landing place, and is

* The reigning prince of Cutch.

occupied by boats of various sizes, some on the stocks, either undergoing repair, or in process of building.

The maritime commerce of Mandavie is important, and boat building is carried on to a considerable extent. The boats are, it is true, of a very rude and primitive construction; but from their remarkable strength, prove admirably adapted for the purposes required. They are half-decked, with broad sterns, high bows, and heavy sails on enormous yards, supported by a stout but clumsy mast, apparently very disproportionate to the size of the craft. The Cutch mariners, however, satisfied with their security, are a most fearless and enterprising race, trading, as their forefathers have done for centuries, to all the ports of the Red Sea, and even stretching out to the eastern coasts of Africa, Ceylon, and the China seas. The exports of Mandavie consist principally of cotton cloths; and in return it receives dates, coffee, dried grapes, antimony, senna, and coloured mats from the ports of the Red Sea; and from Zangibar, on the African coast, elephants' teeth and rhinoceros-horn.

The Cutch moallims or pilots, are singularly intelligent and well informed: they understand the use of the compass, and navigate by charts. Verejee, who is notable amongst them, would have made, with equal advantages of education, a second Anson. He shows you his nautical tables; and his log is as carefully kept as an Indiaman's: he can determine his latitude, and by dead reckoning, his longitude also; and as he unrolls his chart on "Mercator's projection," exultingly points to London, and says, "if you like, I'll pilot you there."

Amongst his books, is a curious old tome, dated MDCCLV., and called the "English Pilot," containing many very quaint remarks "on those things necessary to be known."

The Arab sailors, who, coming from Mocha and other ports of the Red Sea, are frequently seen here, are a wild and singularly picturesque-looking race; and although wearing the flowing robe, and graceful turban, common in the East, seem strikingly dissimilar to the men of other tribes. Their dress is usually of a darker hue, and their pale blue and red turban, less studiously arranged; their complexions are of a deeper hue than even those of the low-caste Hindus; their eyes sparkle with a darker, yet more restless brilliancy, and their general bearing is that of men used to peril, but accustomed to defy it.

Such is a characteristic view of the sea-port of Mandavie, as it first appears to the stranger's eye. The importance of the place being intimately connected with its maritime commerce, much of the bustle and activity of business is to be seen without the walls, although its real wealth and commercial influence exist in the warehouses and granaries of the city, which is surrounded by a strong and well-built wall, having bastions, gates, and wickets. Many of the houses are commodious; some of them built two or three stories high, with terraced roofs and richly carved ornaments; but, in common with those of most native towns, the streets are narrow, dusty, ill ordered, and swarming with Pariah dogs, and fat "bulls of Basan," which lazily stroll about the city, feeding out of the merchants' grain baskets whenever hunger prompts them.

The principal manufacture carried on is the weaving of cotton cloths, of which the makers produce a very tasteful variety: they are woven of various colours, and eminently fanciful designs.

The most strikingly curious object in the city, is a large and well-built palace, most grotesquely ornamented by a variety of carvings, of dancing girls, tigers, and roystering-looking Dutch knaves; each of the men holding a bottle and glass, with a somewhat drunken, but most winning grace. The interior as well as the exterior displays much rich and beautiful carving; but the taste of the designs is evidently European, which seems explained by the story, that the architect, Ram Sing, having been as a child stolen from some part of the Kattywar*

* A large province, separated from Cutch by the gulf of

coast by pirates, was taken by them to Holland, where he became initiated into a knowledge of the fine arts, and returned to decorate his native land. He was the servant of one of the early and most wealthy princes of Cutch, (Rao Lacca,) at whose command he ornamented the province with many specimens of architectural beauty.

This palace, which is used both as a travellers' bungalow and as a residence for invalid officers, is built of white stone, and contains a double suite of capacious rooms; its terraced roof commands an extensive view of the sea, city, and neighbouring country, which is graced by clumps of banyan and palm trees, sheltered villages, and a general appearance of fertility. For this cheerful effect of cultivation, the suburbs of Mandavie are indebted to the Lowannahs,* or agriculturists, who form a numerous caste, and own most of the surrounding villages. Their lands are enclosed, and well irrigated, and the bright green corn waving in the fields, the labouring kine, and the cheerful voices of the husbandmen, give to the open, flat, and otherwise uninteresting country, an appearance of rustic civilization, peculiarly pleasing.

The costume of the Banyans is similar to that

Cutch; it is under our government, but tributary to the Guikwar of Baroda.

† The Lowannahs were originally Sindhians.

of the same caste worn in all parts of India; but the dress of the women is peculiar, tasteful, and highly picturesque. It consists of a satin petticoat, with broad horizontal stripes of red, blue, and yellow, and a bodice tightly covering the bust, and embroidered with various-coloured silks; over the head and shoulders flows the usual "Saree," which, as it gracefully flutters on the breeze, affords a charming effect of grace and softness to the outlines of their elastic figures, whilst the becoming variety of colour selected for their dress, and the brightness of their numerous ornaments, adds gaiety and animation of no common order to the passing scene. On certain holidays, all the women of the city walk together to the sea side in their richest dresses, to render there a votive offering of rice and cocoa-nuts; and on these occasions, the grace and beauty of their persons, the richness and variety of their costume, and the barbaric splendour of their jewels, are shown to the greatest advantage.

The people of Mandavie are a peculiarly handsome race, and much more indebted to nature on this account, than the inhabitants of the interior. I think climate must produce this enviable distinction, the air being agreeably soft and cool; and as a salubrious sea-side residence for invalids, the country is considered superior to any on this side of India. The sands on the shore are firm and equal, extending to a distance of some miles at ebb tide, and affording advantages for a delightful promenade; whilst the soft sand-hillocks nearer the city are overgrown with a hardy species of lilac convolvulus, whose bright leaves serve to conceal the arid soil, and most gratefully refresh the eye. Another material advantage to the convalescent in search of health at Mandavie, is to be found in a change of diet: fish of good quality, amongst which are the much esteemed pomphlet; oysters, crabs, and prawns, abound in the gulf of Cutch; but as the prejudice of the Banyans will not allow fishing to be carried on as a trade, the supply is at times very unequal to the general demand.

At a distance of about two miles inland on the borders of the creek, are the ruins of a city known as "Raipoor," and stated to have once possessed great wealth and importance; but, having fallen under a curse, it became reduced to its present desolate condition. It is supposed to have been the ancient Mandavie,* and to have carried on a flourishing maritime commerce. Coins are found amongst the ruins, bearing the image of an ass; and as the natives can account for so singular an impress, on what was probably the current coin, or for the desertion of the city, only by

* The present Mandavie is in all official documents styled Raipoor.

a "Legend," the tale may be considered worth recording.

LEGEND OF VERE AND VICRAMADITYA, GRANDSONS OF INDRA.

I know not what the truth may be,
I tell the tale as told to me.

The scene opens with Indra, the king of heaven, who amuses himself by seeing four Upsuras* natch before him. His son Gundhurvu-Senu† became enamoured of the surpassing beauty of one of the damsels, and conducted himself so indecorously, that Indra, incensed at his want of delicacy and respect, condemned him to take the form of an ass, and to remain on earth, until, according to the form of the curse, "the smell of the ass's skin, should arise as incense to the throne of heaven." Gundhurvu-Senu was precipitated to the lower world, and found himself close to a poor potter, who was labouring at his vocation in the populous city of Raipoor. The potter was sorely puzzled to guess whence he came; but, seeing he was a good and serviceable ass, he put him into the stables with his other beasts. At night, as the honest potter sat within with his family, he heard a voice from amongst his asses exclaim, "Go to King Dharru, and tell him I demand his daughter in marriage." The

* Celestial courtezans. † The Indian Vulcan.

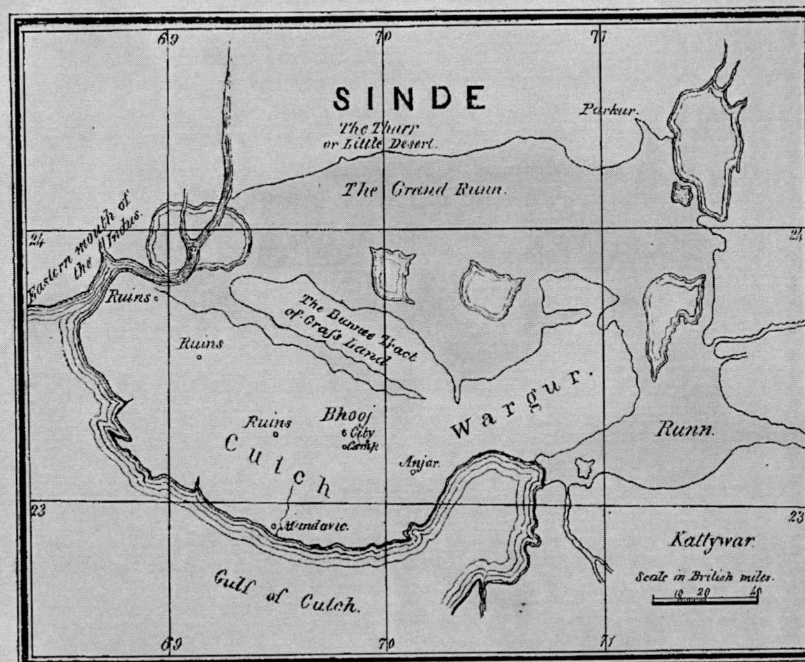

A SKETCH OF CUTCH, THE RUNN, AND COUNTRIES ADJACENT.

From Original Surveys by Capt.ⁿ A. Burnes, F.R.S. &c.

potter with great astonishment identified the speaker, and found him to be the ass he had become so miraculously possessed of, and replied, "What is this, and how can I, who am only a poor potter, speak to a powerful Rajah in behalf of an ass, and how could he give his beautiful daughter in marriage to thee?" Gundhurvu-Senu, however, reiterated his demand, and the fame of it brought crowds of persons, and at length even the king came, to prove the existence of the miracle.

Gundhurvu-Senu related to King Dharru the curse under which he suffered; and as the son of Indra, demanded the princess in marriage, the king hesitated to believe the singular story, and although fearing the anger of Indra might attend his refusal, desired anxiously to save his lovely daughter from so disgusting a marriage. After some reflection King Dharru demanded some proof of his power, and withheld his consent to the alliance, until Gundhurvu-Senu should cause his fort to become iron, its turrets silver, and its gates brass.

Satisfied of the safety of his daughter, King Dharru returned to the city; but as he arose in the morning, great was his dismay, to perceive the strict fulfilment of his demand. To retract was now impossible, and the ceremonies for the marriage of Gundhurvu-Senu with the beautiful daughter of King Dharru, took place with songs, dances, and festivity. The queen, however, shocked at the appearance of the bridegroom, instead of her daughter imposed on him a Loundhi, or waiting woman ; but the son of Indra, who by a modification of the original curse was permitted to doff his ass's hide during the night, appeared with a radiance of such god-like beauty, that the Loundhi found no reason to lament her extraordinary fate. Time passed ; and the queen, unable to gain any explanation from the wife of Gundhurvu-Senu of her apparent indifference to the disgusting form of her husband, stole on their privacy, and, dazzled by his beauty, showed him to her daughter, who became violently enamoured of him. The princess becomes his wife ; but, betraying the secret of Indra's mitigation of his curse to her father, King Dharru, anxious to emancipate his son-in-law, burns the ass's hide. The smoke ascends ; Gundhurvu-Senu is released from the power of the curse, and returns to his father's court. The city which witnessed his disgrace is destroyed, and only these his wives are saved from its population. They travel to a far country, and bring forth two sons, Vere and Vichram, who, after meeting with a variety of adventures, proceed towards Hindustan. Vichram, as he journeys thither, is told in a dream that he will reach a mighty river, down which will float a dead body, bearing on its arm a taweed or charm, which will enable him to become king of Oojein.* Vichram, obeying the injunctions thus communicated, proceeds onwards, and in accordance with the prophetic vision, becomes possessed of the taweed.

On the evening of the brothers' arrival at Oojein, they put up with a potter, whose family were grievously lamenting as for one dead. On inquiring, they learned that the city of Oojein was possessed by a Racus, (or demon,) named Aguah Beytal, and that the people were by turns elected to the supreme power, the Racus devouring, nightly, a king of Oojein. The potter's turn had come, and hence his family's despair. Vichram comforted them, and bade the potter be of good cheer, as he would present himself in his stead. Vichram is accordingly installed king of Oojein, and, at midnight, betakes himself, fully armed, to his sleeping apartment. Aguah Beytal arrived, and, after whetting his appetite with the ghee, rice, and sugar, which were always laid for him, placed himself at the door of Vichram's apartment, and commanded him to come forth. Vichram replied, "Tarry yet awhile; I entreat you to go to the court of Indra, and enquire from Gundhurvu-Senu the age of Vich-

* The capital of the Mahratta possessions.

ram, king of Oojein." Aguah Beytal complied; but, on his return, again urged Vichram to come forth. Vichram, however, entreated him, and said, "Go once again, and beg him to lengthen, only one hour, the ordained life of the King of Oojein." Aguah Beytal returned, saying, "My power is not enough to do this." Then Vichram sprang out, and felled him to the ground, crying out, "Then how canst thou hope to conquer one of godlike origin?" And he commanded Aguah Beytal to depart out of the city; so was Oojein relieved from this dire calamity, and Vichram, being proclaimed king, ruled his people long and peacefully.

Such is the legend; and it will be curious, perhaps, to trace the threads of truth, on which this fabric of nonsense is woven. In Raipoor, or old Mandavie—from which the population was probably dispersed, from the receding of the tides, which made it less advantageous for maritime commerce—the small copper coins are found, called Gundhurvu Pice.*

* It may be observed, that all the Raos of Cutch possess the privilege of striking coins in their own name; consequently, these coins throw much light on the history of ruins

The brilliant reign of Vicramaditya has entitled it to be called the Augustan age of India, and it is known to have been that in which Hindu literature was most cultivated. In Vicramaditya's court were the poets celebrated as the "Nine Gems," and "Calidasi," the chief of these, was the author of "The Fatal Ring," translated by Sir William Jones. Mr. Grant alludes to him in his elegant and learned poem "On the Restoration of Oriental Learning."

"Yet brighter lustres gild Avanti's * towers,
When Vicramadyt sways his subject powers;
See, round his throne, what arts and graces bow!
What virtues diadem his lofty brow!
In sacred band, nine hallowed bards prolong
Unwearied warblings of accordant song!
So move the ninefold spheres their radiant rounds,
With sleepless melodies of angel sounds.
But fancy, chief for Caledasi's muse,
From groves of Indra steals celestial hues,
Hues ever blooming, with whose blushes, sweet,
The immortal Upsurs tinge their snowy feet."

---

in which some of the earlier coinage are found, and are, frequently, the only means by which to judge of their antiquity. The current silver coin is called a Coorie; on one side is the Hindu name of the Rao, and on the reverse, an indistinct Arabic inscription; its value is something less than the fourth of a rupee.

* Oojein — called "Avanti," from "Ava," the Sanskreet word "to preserve."

The reign of Vicramaditya is also the epoch from which, throughout Hindostan and Guzzerat, the natives date. Before the time of this prince, they dated their years from "Pandoo," a rajah of Delhi.—Vicramaditya died B.C. 57.

I fear this may have seemed a very tedious episode to the reader, and I must apologize for having so long detained him from the interior of the province. We will now set out on our journey towards Bhooj; at once the capital of Cutch, and the residence of the British force. It is necessary to travel either on camels, horseback, or in a palankeen, the roads being so rocky in some parts, and so sandy in others, that it is impassable for carriages. The native carts roll and tumble over the ruts, which, by constant labour, their heavy wheels have worn, even on the hardest rocks; but it is done at the imminent peril of the goods they carry; and many a poor traveller, arriving, for the first time, at Bhooj, is condemned to lament over the destruction of his property. Counting the fragments of his china service, he fails not to anathematize, in good set terms, the roads and carts of Cutch, and he casts back a rapid glance on the turnpike roads of Old England, and the spring vans of Messrs. Pickford and Co.

A CUTCH CART.

On the road between Mandavie and Bhooj, Kaira is the only town of any interest—and being remarkable for its manufacture of cotton cloths, may deserve perhaps a rapid sketch. The approach to the town, which is itself situated on the plain, is distinguished by a Mahomedan tomb or temple; which, being erected on a slight elevation, overlooks a fertile and pleasing landscape: in the middle ground, are the fortifications of the old castle, and the foreground is occupied by groups of weavers, busily engaged in weaving a variety of gaily-coloured cloths.

The interior of the temple is decorated with the votive offerings of true believers, and consists of a motley collection of green and white lamps, peacocks' feathers, curiously painted ostrich-eggs, old English looking-glasses, and fringes of coloured beads, that are suspended round a large tomb which occupies the centre of the building. An old Mussulman, in charge of the place, gives flour, and dates, with a few pice,* to all mendicant fakirs.

Kaira has the credit of possessing the prettiest women in Cutch; but I think untruly. The inhabitants are principally weavers and cultivators, apparently remarkable only for poverty and dirt. Like all the daughters of Eve, however, the dam-

* Small copper coin, current in Cutch.

sels of Kaira are not indifferent to the means of personal adornment, and have a peculiar fashion of ornamenting the hems of their garments with a phylacterie of little silver bells ; and decorating their bodices with bits of looking-glass, which are sewn in with the embroidery.

CHAPTER III.

HILL FORT, AND CITY OF BHOOJ.

Distant view of the City.—Snake Tower.—Population.—Sacred Bulls.—Black Buffaloes.—Palace of Rao Daisuljee, Prince of Cutch.—State Elephants.—History and Character of Rao Daisuljee.—Private Reception Chamber of the Rao.—Negro Giant.—State Apartments.—Rao Gore.—Wrestlers.—Garden of the Palace.—Water-works.—Royal Stables.—Kattywar Horses.—Equestrian Appointments.—Native Horsemanship.—Durbar Horsemen.—Custom, or Tenure of "Mohsulsee."—Poorrah Auxiliary Horse.

On passing Kaira, a pretty road leads to the summit of the range of Ghauts which surround the plain, on which is built the city of Bhooj; and the camp, as seen at this distance, looks like a quiet hamlet, sheltered by the hill of Bhoojiah, at the foot of which it rests. The irregularly shaped summit of the hill is crowned with the walls of a fort, which, although not of very imposing magnitude, attract the eye, as an interesting portion of a very pleasing scene.

The hill-forts of India are usually the most picturesque features of its scenery; there is a grandeur in their isolated position and rugged outlines, which carries the mind irresistibly back along the tide of time, and fills it with remembrances of wild and savage beings who made these strong-holds the scenes of tyrant treachery, when might constituted right, and the robber chief, under the protection of these fastnesses, laughed to scorn the fury of the oppressed. Many such are still to be seen in various parts of India, frowning in their gloomy might over gay and smiling valleys; and wild tales, and spirit-stirring traditions, are told of the daring and violent men, who, sweeping from their louring portals with a fierce and warlike train, ravaged the fair plains, plundered the helpless, and returned in triumph, to enjoy the fruit of their devastation.

On a nearer view, the Hill Fort of Bhoojiah has little which can entitle it to share in this romantic interest. The elevation of the hill is inconsiderable, and the fort does not promise a very secure retreat. At one angle of the wall, is a small square tower, dedicated to the worship of the Cobra Capella. The peculiar ceremonies connected with this worship I shall have occasion to describe elsewhere.

The city of Bhooj is about a mile from the British camp, and surrounded by a strong and well-built wall; it is said to contain about 30,000 inhabitants. The streets are narrow, dirty, and rendered almost impassable by herds of sacred bulls, who are here, as in all other Hindu towns, a type of the well-being, ease, and indolence of the priesthood. The black buffaloe is also a frequenter of native towns; and, forming not unusually (like the Irish pig) the sole property of its owner, is cared for as a source of wealth and comfort. At sunset, being driven from the pastures into the city, it either lingers near its home, roams about the streets, or lies like a mud heap in the path. It is not only in a passive state, however, that these animals are dangerous and offensive by their right of liberty. Quiet as is their general deportment, the spirit of hilarious mirth sometimes breaks out amongst them, when three or four may be encountered butting, whirling, and racing through the streets, their tails horizontally extended, covering the bystanders with dust, upsetting the merchants' grain-baskets, throwing down the luckless and denuded children, and scattering confusion on every side.

The most interesting and important object in the city, is the palace of His Highness Rao Daisuljee, the ruling prince of Cutch. It is a large white stone building, decorated with beautiful carvings, and fine fretwork, in the same style as the ornaments of the palace at Mandavie. These, being more modern than the rest of the building, were probably added by Ram Sing. The inner courts of the palace are gained through a number of passages and gateways occupied by

Arab guards, and decorated with their weapons. At the entrance of the first gate are kept his highness' state elephants, which are tattooed and painted in the most approved style of native taste. On state occasions they form part of the procession which attends the Rao; it is usual for them to precede his highness, and they are taught, when marshalled on one side, to salute him with a loud trumpet as he passes. It is well known that state elephants are as necessary to the pomps of an Eastern prince, as jewels to the regalia of a European monarch. The Rao of Cutch, however, is a poor prince, and owns but few.

Having now arrived at the foot of the flight of steps, which lead from the great court-yard to the private apartments of his highness, let us, before we ascend them, take a rapid view of the past history of this palace, and become in some degree acquainted with the character of its present master. In recalling the historical records connected with this spot, we feel how fearful it is, to contemplate the hideous effects of power, when immersed in sensuality. We will, therefore, pass over the scenes of bloodshed and violence, so monstrous in their deformity, of which this spot has been made the theatre, by preceding princes of this unhappy country, which has been equally torn by civil feuds, and harassed and impoverished by its rulers.

HIS HIGHNESS THE RAO OF CUTCH.

During the present reign, Cutch has regained its early tranquillity, and the country, from having been ravaged by freebooters and outlaws, is restored to the enjoyment of a legitimate and peaceful government.

The present Prince Rao Daisuljee, is not more than twenty-two years of age, having been elected on the formal deposition of his father, Rao Bharmuljee, a prince long rendered infamous by his public and private crimes. The manners of the young Rao are peculiarly urbane and amiable; the personal attachment of his dependants is a proof of his benevolence and kindness of disposition; and the respect he observes in public towards his unhappy father, evinces the delicacy and tenderness of his character. The studies of his Highness were early directed to the acquirement of the English language, literature, and sciences; but before his knowledge of either became sufficient to influence his opinions or regulate his tastes, the political dissensions of the petty chiefs of Cutch rendered it imperative that power should at once be vested in the appointed successor of their deposed sovereign, although he had not yet attained his majority. Since that period, the cares of government have occupied the young prince's attention too fully, to permit any progress to be made in the cultivation of his early pursuits; and his knowledge is consequently very limited.

D

Without any efforts having been made to instil the principles of the Christian creed into the mind of his Highness, it would be difficult to state what are his peculiar religious tenets. His mother, to whom he was most tenderly attached, was a devout supporter of the Brahminical creed; and it is supposed, skilfully adapting all her topics of persuasion to his youthful understanding, has succeeded in embuing his mind with the darkest superstitions of his people. The population of Cutch, however, being composed of nearly an equal proportion of Mahomedans and Hindus, the interests of his government require, that he should conform in public to both these forms of worship; but it is probable, that he retains only a heartfelt respect for that religion, whose tenets are identified with the affections and associations of his childhood.

In person the Rao is remarkably stout, with peculiarly fine eyes, and a benevolent and agreeable expression of countenance, although unfortunately disfigured by the ravages of small-pox. His dress is usually rich, well arranged, and strikingly picturesque. On state occasions it consists of a most magnificent Kinkaul turban, of the usual stupendous size worn by the Rajpoots,*

* The form, size, and material of native turbans vary with the rank and caste of the wearer; but none are of so enormous a size as those of the Rajpoots. Of their common dimensions

ornamented with strings of pearl, and jewels of great value, with immense ear-rings of gold wire set with precious stones. Over the muslin Ankriha,* worn by all natives of respectability, his Highness has a sort of body armour of thickly wadded purple velvet embroidered with gold; a pair of rich satin trousers, also embroidered or rather embossed with gold; and crimson velvet slippers, curved upwards at the front, and decorated with pearls and coloured silks.

His Highness's jewels are of great price, and very numerous; consisting principally of armlets, bracelets, taweeds* and a succession of rings and necklaces of which it would be hopeless to attempt a description. The gems most in use are pearls, rubies, and diamonds, but uncut, and set in the rudest style of workmanship. His Highness has some knowledge of the English language; and it is the custom for the European officers stationed in Cutch, to make him visits of ceremony, with which he seems gratified, and has in several cases evinced a warm friendship and interest for some, with whom circumstances have

some idea may be gained from the fact, that an English gentleman remarking with unfeigned astonishment, the size of one worn by the Rao's prime minister, he was answered by that worthy functionary, "Oh! this is nothing, it only weighs fifteen pounds," (Punderah seer kè puggre.)

* Body cloth. † Charms.

connected him.* Natives of respectability visit him constantly, and once a month he holds a

* For the subjoined additional notice of his Highness, the Rao of Cutch, the writer is indebted to the pen of a friend :—"Daisuljee, the present Rao of Cutch, was installed as monarch of his country in July 1834, at which period, although not of age, he was considered capable by the British Government of taking upon himself the responsibility of office. His father Bharmuljee was, for a series of crimes, and a life of debauchery and wickedness, without any attention whatever to the welfare of his kingdom, deposed whilst the present Rao was yet an infant; the government of the country being in the meantime carried on by a regency, the head of which was the British Resident and representative at the court. The education of the young Rao being thus entrusted to the British Government, they determined to give him the advantage of a more enlightened one than falls to the lot of many Asiatics, especially of the regal caste; for this end, the Reverend Mr. Gray, then chaplain at Bhooj, was selected as being well qualified for the office of instructor to the young prince. Death unfortunately intervened to prevent his accomplishing the task he had commenced; but in the person of Lieut. (now Captain) Crofton of H. M.'s 6th Royals, a most able and assiduous seconder of Mr. Gray's intentions was found; and under the able tuition and good management of this gifted and accomplished young officer, Daisuljee was pronounced, at nineteen, perfectly capable of mounting the throne of his father, and of healing the wounds which under Bharmuljee's tyrannical reign his subjects had received. The love the Cutchees bore to the young prince was enthusiastic, and his brother Jharrejahs, or chiefs, of Cutch unanimously greeted him on his accession to the throne, as head of the Bhyaud, or brotherhood, and swore eternal allegiance to him. The installation was a very interesting scene; and as the British

Durbar,* when persons of all ranks have access to his presence. It is customary for such to bring limes, cocoa nuts, &c., which they lay at the Rao's feet, with expressions of allegiance and respect. The Durbar is held on the day of the new moon, but is sometimes convoked for the purposes of council, at other times.

We will now enter the palace, and, accompanied by his Highness, who feels great delight in displaying its curiosities to his English visitors, we will traverse his lofty and gaily decorated apartments.

Government had been the real guardian of Daisuljee, to whom he owed his education and elevation, all due honor was done by the British officers on the occasion, and gratefully and graciously acknowledged by the Rao. The Resident, Colonel Pottinger, as a finishing stroke to the acts of the British Government, seated the young prince on the throne, bound some splendid jewels (the gift of Lord Clare) on his turban, presented him with a letter of friendship from the governor (Lord Clare,) and saluted him as Rao of Cutch, the artillery in camp firing a royal salute on the occasion. Great were the feasting and general joy on that day.

"In stature Daisuljee is rather low, and very much inclined to obesity; his disposition is extremely amiable, and his manners frank and very like those of a European. He converses in English fluently—perhaps the only Asiatic prince who does—and is well informed on most subjects. His age is about twenty-two, but he looks at least twenty eight."

* A levee, or place in which a native prince holds his council, receives visits, or administers justice.

The Rao is usually found seated in his private reception-chamber, a small room, the walls of which are hung with swords, shields, matchlocks, and a curious variety of other weapons, of which his Highness seems most to value a beautifully inlaid gun, presented to him by Sir John Malcolm, on his visit to Cutch in 1830. During his hours of relaxation from the cares of business, the Rao is frequently attended by a negro giant, a sort of royal jester, who throws himself into all sorts of contortions, and displays an agility in the performance of his antics, which excites the risible faculties of his Highness to their greatest extent, keeping him in a convulsion of laughter at the monster's efforts.

The public apartments of the palace consist of the Hall of Audience, in which the Durbars are held, the State Apartment, and the Furwaneh Khana, or Hall of Fountains. The last of these, which contains a great number of jets-d'eau, is set apart for the exhibition of water-works, and on the festivals of the Dussorah, Dewallah, &c., is brilliantly illuminated. Adjoining this hall, and leading from it by a richly ornamented door, is the State Apartment, which, in fact, is a small room, contained in the centre of a saloon of large dimensions; and, being the very core of the palace, forms its sanctum, or most venerated spot. It is about eight feet square, and its chief ornament is a state-bed, bearing the richly gemmed sword of Rao Gore, a cruel and profligate prince, who succeeded his father, Rao Lacca, in the government of Cutch, in the year 1760. Rao Gore was accustomed to use this apartment during his hours of pleasurable relaxation, and to his taste it is indebted for its singular decorations.

In order to preserve the dignity of this spot, the present Rao visits it at stated periods, with an appearance of some ceremony, and much true respect; on the occasion of our visit he accompanied us as *cicerone*.

Feeling quite inadequate to the task of presenting the reader with a *catalogue raisonné* of all the unnameable articles of *virtù*, which adorn this chosen retreat of luxurious royalty, I must request him to imagine himself introduced, by some wholesale glass-dealer, to his sample room, where, amongst jelly glasses, and old vases, are introduced some half dozen antique musical clocks, all playing at once, and the whole display brilliantly illuminated by large wax candles, at noon-day! This mental picture may then afford him some idea of the motley and incongruous *mélange* of ornament, which contributes to the regal magnificence of this most dazzling of state-apartments. The presence of the clocks, some antique pictures, a celestial and a terrestrial globe, are attributed to the redoubtable Ram Sing, who is said to have brought them with him from Holland. The hall which encloses this singular apartment, is ornamented by a succession of pillars, pier-glasses, and pictures in rich and massy frames. The floor is remarkably unpleasant to walk on, being inlaid with a sort of small Dutch tile. The roof and pillars are decorated with rich gold mouldings, and other ornaments, much too faded to afford material for description; and the small compartments between them are supplied with fittings of triangularly shaped looking-glass. The pictures, which nearly cover the walls, are either horrible copies, or the worst possible prints, from the old English and Dutch masters. Amongst them are, Hogarth's "Rake's Progress," — sundry portraits of Lady Carteret, in stomacher and *toupée*—with here and there a dismal-looking shepherdess, or a snuff-coloured *belle* of the Rao's own family, executed by a Chinese artist. On leaving these apartments, and returning to the Hall of Audience,—"Will't please you to go see the wrestlers," is, in other words, the Rao's general invitation to his guests; and he at once leads them to a carpeted and draperied balcony, looking over the courts of the palace, which are crowded by anxious spectators. Behind his Highness's chair stand slaves, gracefully waving punkahs of ostrich and peacock's feathers round his superbly ornamented turban; and below him are ranged the wrestlers, fine Rajpoots, in the prime of life, displaying a symmetry of form and a development of muscular power, not unworthy the gymnasium theatres of ancient Greece. If we except one long waving lock of hair, their heads were closely shaven, and their only covering a pair of crimson silk drawers, descending about half-way to the knee, and bound tightly round the loins with a many-coloured scarf.

After a succession of salaams to the Rao, two of the wrestlers step forward, and the exhibition commences, by each violently slapping the inside of his arms and thighs, in succession, with the open palm of the opposite hand; until, at an understood signal, the men seize each other by the waist, place their foreheads together, and struggle, toss, and twist each other about, until one falls; when the victor, cheered by the shouts of the spectators, gracefully lifts a handful of dust to his forehead, and salaaming to the Rao, backs to his place, while another pair step forward, to repeat the same ceremony.

This slight sketch will convince the reader that there was little here to awaken classical reminiscences, or to associate the Rajpoot wrestlers of his Highness of Cutch, with the Athletæ of the Stadium; yet, meagre as it was, the display seemed eminently attractive to the crowd around us, who rent the air with shouts of applause, and evinced the most barbarous and unfeigned delight during the combats.

After this exhibition, his Highness led us to his garden, which is half filled with the white Mogree,* plantain-trees, and poppies. These last seem chosen for the royal garden, rather from the rich and glowing tints they display, so much in accordance with the native taste, than for their medicinal qualities, although his Highness eagerly reminded me of them, as we passed. This garden introduces us to the Rao's favourite retreat, which is a large tank, surrounded by alcoves, from which he enjoys the cool breeze, diversified by the amusement of watching the bright water fling up its sparkling spray from a jet in the centre. The machinery of this is clumsy, and ill-managed, so that, long ere we could imagine ourselves listening to the gentle voice of "Zorahayda," from beside the Moorish fountain, or indulge in any reverie of romance, we were condemned to see half a dozen stalwart natives, in the most primitive *déshabillé*, dash into the tank, tugging ropes and pipes behind them, which, after much time, great labour, and abundant vociferation, were duly attached to the main pipe, and the

* A sweetly scented plant, somewhat resembling jasmine.

water fell over in sparkling showers, to the unbounded delight of the aforesaid watermen.

In the court-yard of the palace, are the royal stables, containing a stud of about five hundred horses, of which the Rao is particularly fond: most of them are of the large Kattywar breed, with long tails, which are dyed red, in accordance with the native taste. The Rao's favourite riding-horses are of a dun colour, and a bay, which, on state occasions, are most splendidly decorated by a number of massive, and richly chased plates, of fine Venetian gold, set on the bridle, crupper, martingale, &c. The saddle in common use is an iron frame-work, rising behind and before in high peaks, frequently gaily painted, or, amongst persons of wealth, formed wholly of chased gold and silver. These saddles are covered with a profusion of gilded satin, rich housings, and picturesquely embroidered cloth covers, which produce a seat so luxurious, that the peculiar amble of the well-trained horses can hardly be perceptible to the rider. In lieu of leathern bridles, they use thick crimson silk cords attached to the severe Mahratta bit, and decorate the embroidered head-stalls with a profusion of the small shells called cowries, variously coloured beads, silk tassels, &c.

The large breed of Kattywar horses are well adapted, from their size and figure, to display this finery to the best effect; and although lacking the symmetry of form and high blood of the Arab, are fine animals, and capable of great exertion.

One of the great characteristics of the East, is the skill the natives display in horsemanship ; to the "desert-born" his horse and spear are at once his protection and his only property. Far from the tents of his tribe, the Arab has no friend but his faithful steed, no home but his saddle; he has no means of defence or support, but such as are afforded him by the fleetness of his horse, and the strength of his own right hand, and ready spear. In the East, the horse takes the legitimate place his noble nature deserves in creation's scale ; he is here the companion and faithful friend of man ; he bears him gallantly on to daring exploits ; shares with him the humble meal, and the ball of opium ;* rests by his master's side as he sleeps under the broad shade of some spreading palm, on the cool borders of a tank, and leaves the drudgery of bearing heavy burdens of merchandize, to the camel, the bullock, and the ass.

Belonging to the Cutch Durbar, are a few horsemen, irregulars, in the service and pay of his

* A modern oriental traveller has stated, that after a fatiguing march, when man and horse were both well nigh exhausted, his guide dismounted, and, after smoking his hookah for a few minutes, divided his pill of opium with his horse; after which, both completed a farther march of thirty miles, without any appearance of fatigue.

Highness the Rao, whose dress and appointments are singularly picturesque. They wear the Cutchee turban, which is very large and heavy ;* and their outer coat is generally thickly quilted, and lined with cotton. They are armed with a matchlock, sword, spear, and shield; the last of which is made of clear rhinoceros hide, bossed with gold or silver. Over their saddle, is thrown a huge leathern cover, finished at the corners by large tassels, and having pockets in front, into which the horseman puts his chillum,† his opium, and the food for his steed; and thus appointed, they will travel over the country for days, or weeks, without any other refreshment than is afforded by the little store in their saddle bags; proving

> "With how small allowance,
> Untroubled nature doth herself suffice."

The Rao, on occasions of ceremony, is generally attended by about five hundred of these men, whose appearance, with that of elephants, banners, and other insignia of Eastern royalty, produces a picturesque and splendid, if not an absolutely imposing effect.

* As it has been remarked, the Cutchees, and all Rajpoots, are noted for the amplitude of their turbans and beards. The latter they constantly dye with a preparation of indigo; it being a trait of Eastern dandyism to keep them black, even when age may have turned them grey.

† Small hookah.

Barvajee, one of the most distinguished of these Grassia* chieftains, is connected by blood with the Rao. He is a remarkably fine man, possessing in common with the rest of his tribe a most dignified carriage, with great *hauteur* of manner. The Rao himself is one of the Bhyaud, or brotherhood, better known by the title of Jharrejah.†

In connection with the duties of these retainers of his Highness, is a singular custom called Mohsulsee. The Rao, when he may happen to require submission from a Rajpoot‡ chief to any particular demand, notifies the same to the party; when, if uncomplied with, his Highness sends a horseman to the particular town or village governed by the rebellious chief, who is compelled by original contract to pay whatever fine

* "Grassia" is another term for the description of feudal tenure mentioned in the note below.

† For explicit accounts of the Rajpoots, their quixotic notions of family dignity, &c., *vide* SIR JOHN MALCOLM'S *Central India*, or TOD'S *Rajpootana*.

‡ Cutch is governed on precisely the same feudal system, as existed in England, during the reign of the Norman conqueror; and the Rajpoot or Jharrejah chiefs of Cutch hold their lands on the same description of tenure, as our English nobles did at that time, their immunities and privileges being similar; they are bound to afford military service to the Rao, upon requisition, and by a breach of this contract, forfeit their rights.

per diem his Highness may choose to levy, until the demand is complied with. The servant of the Rao who levies the fine, is called a Mohsul. There is no fixed amount of tax; this depends on the will of the enforcing authority, and is usually regulated by the urgency of the case. The highest fine which I believe has been levied in Cutch, was twenty coories* a-day; but in the province of Kattywar, where Mohsuls are even more used than in Cutch, a fine was levied on the Jam of Noanugger, of five hundred rupees a-day. The case, however, seems to have been considered insufficient to authorize the imposition of this immense fine, as it was levied only to compel the prince to produce some papers, connected with a trifling pecuniary dispute.

A small proportion of the Poorrah auxiliary horse are also, in Cutch, under the command of two European officers. They are a fine race of men, chiefly Patans,† and wear a very gay, and pretty green and crimson uniform, not unlike the greenwood dress of the merry archers of Sherwood. In lieu, however, of the widely flapping beaver and heron plume, these warriors don a crimson turban, the folds of which, after being twisted in a sort of trellis pattern round the head,

* About six rupees.

† High-caste men from Delhi.

pass under the chin, and render it secure. These men are always well mounted; they carry a carbine instead of spear; and are more military in their general bearing than the Durbar horsemen.*

Of the Seyed† mercenary soldiers in the pay of the Rao the annexed plate will be found to convey an accurate idea. It is the portrait of an enormously bulky man, six feet two inches in height. The Rao of Cutch musters about five or six hundred mounted soldiers, armed and accoutred in this style. The curiously shaped articles in red, are powder-horn, and pouches for the matchlock—a most unwieldly and inconvenient sort of fire-arm. Such, however, is the prejudice in favour of old customs and things amongst these people, that they will not adopt the evidently far superior kind of weapon used by Europeans, although they daily witness its advantages. Nor can they plead inability to procure it; since there are *lookars* (workers in iron) in the city of Bhooj, who are capable of turning out a flint or even a percussion lock, which many an Englishman would not be ashamed to own as his production. But

* These Durbar horsemen have their horses found them by the Rao, from whom they also receive a coorie a day, and a small quantity of grain; it is usual to give grain in some cases in lieu of wages.

† "Seyed" signifies a priest of the Mahomedan persuasion.

their conceit is on a par with their blind ignorance and infatuation.

The saddle-cloth is of thin leather; and underneath it every soldier carries his own and his horse's provisions for a day's march, head and heel ropes, and leathern feeding-bag; so that a few minutes' time is sufficient for a man to prepare for a march of a hundred miles. These troops are very useful for the service required of them; but, of course, not to be put in competition with a regular body of cavalry. In certain cases, however, the latter would be utterly useless, whilst our "mercenary friends" would "do the state some service."

CHAPTER IV.

THE HAREM.

Wives of the Rao.—Guard of Eunuchs.—The Author's Visit. — Dowry of the Ladies.—The Rao's Mother.—Beauty of the Soodah Women. — Costume of the Queen Mother. — Jewels of the Ranees. — Etiquette of Departure. — Moral and Intellectual state of Women in the East.

"Shawls, the richest of Cashmere,
Pearls from Oman's Bay are here;
And Golconda's royal mine
Sends her diamonds here to shine."

HIS Highness the Rao of Cutch has five wives,* who reside in a wing of the palace, separated from the main building by several court-yards and passages. The avenue immediately leading to the women's apartments is guarded at its entrance by a pair of most hideous eunuchs, who sit cross-legged, in a sort of basket chair placed

* His Highness is about to form an alliance with two more women, the daughter of powerful chiefs, who esteem it a high honour to gain admission for their offspring to the Royal Harem. The Rao most sensibly regrets the existence of this characteristic custom of his country; but conforms to it from

on each side of the portal. These sooty guardians of female virtue are armed to the teeth, and in addition to that, have a huge blunderbuss lying by each seat. Having passed these retainers of marital tyranny, we enter the large court, filled on the occasion of my visit to the ladies, by about three hundred women of the city, of various castes and degrees, who had come to gratify two of the strongest desires of the female mind, curiosity and gossip. After passing up an avenue, formed by a double file of these dark beauties,—

"Maidens, in whose orient eyes
More than summer sunshine lies,"—

and being greeted by whisperings, gigglings, and other demonstrations of amusement, at what they thought remarkable in my dress and manner, I entered the sitting apartment of the Ranees,* which was a stone verandah, level with, and open to the court, having sleeping-rooms, and other private apartments, leading from doors to the back.

policy, and as a means of securing peace with the neighbouring provinces;

"For all the amours of princes are,
But guarantees of peace or war."

The Rao, on his marriage, presents the bride with a village, as her dowry: the produce of this is considered sufficient for her expenses, and whatever presents the Rao afterwards bestows on her, are as instances of his favour.

* Wives of the Rao.

The Rao's mother, who resides with her husband the ex-Rao in a separate palace, came to her son's harem on the occasion of my visit, and received me with great ease, partaking of the graces of European etiquette. Taking my hand, she expressed her pleasure at seeing me, and then placing me in a chair next her own, conversed agreeably on a variety of subjects, in excellent Hindustanee. She is a very lovely woman, and does not appear older than about five and thirty; she has a very fair complexion, fine figure, and lustrous black eyes; not possessing the languid sleepy softness, which generally characterizes the native eye, but large, bright, and expressive. She is the daughter of a chief of Soodahs, a tribe who inhabit the great desert of the Thurr,* and are remarkable for the surpassing beauty of their women. The fathers of these belles calculate their amount of property according to their "heads of daughters," being happy to dispose of them as brides to the highest bidder.† And to judge of all, by this specimen in the person of the lovely queen-mother, "if lusty love would go in quest of beauty," few of the daughters of the

* The great desert which bounds Cutch to the north, beyond the salt tract of the Runn.

† The Jharrejah or Rajpoot chiefs usually intermarry with the Soodah women, as they can do so without offence to their pride of caste.

land could, I think, compete with the passing fairness of the Soodah maidens.

The Ranee,

> "Rich in the gems of India's gaudy zone,"

was superbly attired according to the fashions of Mandavie, which have been before described; but the materials of her dress were unusually costly and well chosen. Her petticoat was of a rich Tyrian purple satin, embossed, with a border, and scattered bunches of flowers; each flower being formed of various gems, and the leaves and stems richly embroidered in gold and coloured silks. Her bodice was of the same material as the petticoat, having the form of the bosom marked by circular rows of seed pearl; her slippers were of embroidered gold, open at the heels, and curved up towards the instep in front; from her graceful head flowed a Kinkaub scarf, woven from gold thread of the finest texture and most dazzling brightness. Her soft glossy hair, parted in the Greek style, was confined by a golden fillet, and a profusion of pearl ornaments; and on her brow, imbedded in the delicate flesh, and apparently unsecured by any other means, rested a beautiful star of diamonds and pearls.*

The lovely Ranee was absolutely laden with

* The arrangement of diamonds, rubies, and pearls, in alternate circles, is their favourite style for setting ornaments; at least, I saw no other.

jewels: A description of her nose-ring, ear-rings, toe-rings, finger-rings, armlets, bracelets, anklets, and necklaces, would alone occupy a volume.

The young Ranees, the present Rao's wives, were seated together on a mat in a remote corner of the verandah, decked in all their finery; but the poor girls, abashed and timid, sat huddled together, afraid to be seen, yet every moment whispering to each other, with a half suppressed giggle; now and then stealing a glance at me through their long eye-lashes, but turning their eyes away the instant the gesture was observed, and hiding their pretty faces in the laps of their companions. By degrees, however, they gained courage; gave me their trinkets to admire; asked me a variety of trifling questions; insisted on handling all the ornaments I wore, and would, I believe, have fairly undressed me, had I not avoided any farther familiarity, by re-commencing a conversation with the fascinating queen mother.

The jewels of the young Ranees were similar to those already described; but one of the fair dames seemed peculiarly enchanted with the beauty of a ring she wore on her first finger. It was indeed of huge dimensions; in the centre was a mirror about the size of a half crown piece, and this was encircled with rubies, pearls, and diamonds. The fair wearers of all this barbaric wealth must have been sorely wearied ere the day was done, had not female vanity aided them to support its burthen; their ear-rings alone were of solid gold, and not less than eight inches each in diameter,* and embossed with gems of a large size.

The Ranees have no family; they are all very young, and seem perfectly happy together, and contented with their lot.

After spending some time with the Ranees, who expressed great anxiety to hear of other English ladies who had visited them at various times, I made a movement for taking leave; when two slave girls entered, bearing trays, on which were little baskets formed of leaves, and containing betel-nuts, pān supairee, cinnamon, and other spices, with rose-water, attar, and sandal wood oil in minute opal vases. The Rao's mother then presented me with betel-nut, which in Eastern etiquette is understood to convey a permission to depart; and having (as a mark of friendship) sprinkled me, by means of a little golden ladle, with the various unguents, accompanied by a profuse shower of rose-water, scattered through the rose of a richly gemmed Golaubdani,† the Ranees all politely and kindly entreated me to

* From positive measurement:—these enormous pendants are supported by small gold hooks, which fasten into the hair above the ear.

† A Persian bottle for holding rose-water.

repeat my visit. Afterwards, each took my hand and raised it smilingly and gracefully to her forehead. I then left them, and was ushered back through the wondering crowd to the outer gate of the palace.

The situation of the Ranees interested me deeply. I was pleased with their amiability, but felt sincere commiseration for their degraded, useless, and demoralizing condition. These poor girls are permitted the free association of numerous beings of their own sex, all equally ignorant, and many of them far more evil in their nature: they are themselves the slaves of a web of circumstances, woven round their lives by a long and systematic practice of jealous tyranny, and a series of debasing customs, from the social injustice of which the mind of every liberal observer must recoil, when he reflects that the same beings whose moral and rational qualities are thus restricted have, notwithstanding, displayed an energy of mind, determination of purpose, and a cunning aptitude for political intrigue, which, originating in the recesses of the harem, has spread anarchy over kingdoms and deluged them with blood. If, in a state of real ignorance, and apparently habitual apathy, the women of the East display at times so much natural capacity, and mental energy, why, it may reasonably be asked, should they not be equally capable of receiving intellectual culture, and by the consequent development of their faculties and feelings, be prepared for, and permitted to take the part of real usefulness and responsibility in social life, which nature designed in the creation of woman? This question, however, can be only answered by the consideration of others, involving matters of great political interest. The emancipation of Eastern women from their present mental and personal imprisonment, would require that the prejudices of their forefathers should be laid low, and that the great spirit of change should move over their political, moral, and religious institutions, sweeping away the dust of ages, and erecting toleration as the emblem of awakening truth, over the fallen fanes of heathen worship.

To effect this, a series of renovating circumstances must produce opinions very far in advance of those which now bow down the intellects of this benighted people; and whether it be consistent with the objects of British power in India, to introduce wise means conducive to such improvement, I leave to the conscientious consideration of those, whose information, talents, and position afford them peculiar advantage for forming a just estimate of the probable gain, but the certain risk, of any attempt to raise the people of India from beneath the yoke of their prejudices, by cultivating their faculties, imbuing them with knowledge, and softening their hearts with all the nameless graces of civilization.

Should the political aspect of Indian affairs ever render such a course advisable in the opinion of our rulers, many years must yet roll on before the darkest institutions of heathenism shall vanish at the bright day-spring of improvement; and until then, the poor Hindu woman must be content to remain, during life, the debased slave of her master's will, and at his death, be doomed, in accordance with immemorial usage, to yield her life by cruel torture, a sacrifice to the fanatic faith of her country, and the rapacious wickedness of the Brahminical priesthood;—who will thus continue to deceive their miserable votaries,

> "With gay religions, full of pomp and gold,
> And devils to adore for deities."

CHAPTER V.

HINDU TOMBS.

Effects of an Earthquake.—Centre Tomb.—Tomb of the Wives of Rao Rahiden.—Atonement of the Rao for his temporary Conversion to Mahomedanism.

A GROUP of very beautiful tombs built of red sand-stone, and very richly and curiously decorated, forms the principal ornament of the sterile plain of Bhooj. The tombs are situated on the borders of a fine tank near the walls of the city; but are visible from all parts of the neighbourhood. Many of them were materially injured by the effects of an earthquake in 1819. The shafts of some of the columns are rent, and the capitals of others are now lying on the ground in a state of decay and confusion; yet the effect of their architectural beauty is uninjured, and the crumbling fragments of richly carved figures, cornices, and pillars which lie around, are not, as monuments of art, less interesting and attractive to the eye of taste, because the tender herb, and the wild flower, spring from their fissures "on the grassy soil."

The centre tomb is least injured. It was erected by Rao Gore in honour of his father, Rao Lacca, in 1760; and as the province of Cutch was at its zenith of wealth and power during the reign of Rao Lacca's father (Daisul) this may account for the erection of so costly and splendid a cenotaph. It is a polygonally shaped building, having two entrances, and a sort of gallery round it; the roof of which is curiously and beautifully carved, and supported by a pillar at every angle. This encloses a small room, in which were originally deposited the royal ashes, and sixteen rude and upright stones daubed with a pigment of red ochre, representing the Rao's wives, who performed suttee at his decease. Report, indeed, affirms that the ladies of the harem substituted slave-girls in their place; but as this is not usually permitted, I should doubt the truth of the assertion. The tomb is decorated by the before-mentioned Ram Sing; but the style of the figures is not so essentially Dutch, as those which form the ornaments of his other works. They consist principally of representations of Nātch girls, men playing on the siringa, elephants, alligators, and Hunaman, the monkey god.

The beautifully wrought traceries of flowers, which ornament the friezes, mouldings, and capitals of the numerous columns—the variety of subjects introduced to decorate this great monument of labour and ingenuity—seem to defy even a complete observation. During a lengthened residence in its neighbourhood, this tomb has constantly been a subject of curiosity and admiration to me as a work of art; and at every visit, I find renewed cause for surprise at the ingenuity of its architect.

At a short distance from this beautiful edifice is a second tomb, much smaller, but still endued with historical interest. It was erected by the wives of Rao Rahiden as an expiation for his having allowed his mind to be converted to Mahomedanism. The death of this prince caused a feud between the Hindu and Mogul population of Cutch: the latter insisted on burying his body, by right of the Rao's known conversion; but the Hindus, at the instance of the ladies of the harem, seized the body on its way to sepulture, and burnt it with great pomp. Long after this time, his ashes were removed from the tomb, and carried by the Brahmins to the Ganges,* as a yet higher act of atonement.

* In India it is customary to commit the ashes of the dead to the sacred waters, as an act of merit. And here they have rivers of it, instead of mere vases blessed in St. Peter's. Of these, the Ganges is considered the most desirable, although the Krishna, and many others, have no small reputation for holiness.

CHAPTER VI.

SUTTEE.

Recent Suttee in Cutch.—Immemorial usage.—Tests of Conjugal Affection from the Shastrus.—Description of the Pyre.—Apparent apathy of the Widow.—Address of Captain Burnes.—Devotion and Heroism of the Victim.—Suffocation.—Hindu Belief.—Monuments of Suttee.—Censurable Conduct of the Rao.—Self-immolation of a Female Water-bearer, on the Death of the Rao's Mother.—Effects of Popular Superstition.—Means of eluding British Authority.—Alternative Penances.

" As the snake-catcher draws the serpent from his hole, so she, rescuing her husband (from hell,) rejoices with him." *Hindu Shastrus.*

AMONGST all the rites connected with the Hindu creed, none have perhaps been so fully known to the European world through the medium of description as that most inhuman one, of the self-cremation of Hindu widows. In the British territories the act is forbidden; but it still, alas! too frequently occurs, where the native power is most influential. As the manner of rendering this dreadful oblation varies in different districts, I will record the circumstances connected with a Suttee which lately took place in Cutch: the province being under Native Government, its people acted in perfect independence of our control.

The inducements to the performance of this ceremony are drawn from immemorial usage, founded on the denouncements and promises of the sacred writings of the Hindus. From the authority of Sanscreet works, it appears, that the sacrifice may be made, either as an expiation for the sins of the deceased, or in the hope of its entitling the victim to eternal felicity, as will be seen from the following extracts :*—

"Dying with her husband, she sanctifies her maternal and paternal ancestors."

Again—

"Such a wife, adoring her husband, in celestial felicity with him, greatest, most admired ; with him, she shall enjoy the delights of heaven, while fourteen Indras reign."

Also—

"Though her husband had killed a Brahmana, broken the ties of gratitude, or murdered his friend, she expiates the crime."

The woman whose sacrifice I am about to describe was of high caste, the only wife of Bhoojray, a man possessing some power and

* From a paper in the Asiatic Researches, by H. Colebrook, Esq.

much wealth in the province, and an intimate and confidential friend of the Rao. During the latter days of his life, his wife declared her intention of performing suttee at his death, which being made known to the British Resident, he immediately requested the Rao to use his influence with the woman, when she became a widow, to prevent the completion of her design. When the time arrived, his Highness sent for the woman, expostulated with her, and offered her protection, both in his own name, and in that of the British Government, but found her determination unalterable ; and the widow left the palace, to prepare by prayer and purification for the intended sacrifice. The following morning being appointed for burning the body of the deceased Bhoojray, a funeral pyre was erected immediately in front of Rao Lacca's tomb : it was formed of long bamboos, the tops of which being forced into the ground in a circle, the upright ends were confined together in the form of a bee-hive, and covered with thorns, and dried grass ; the entrance was through a small aperture, left open on one side.

News of the widow's intentions having spread, a great concourse of people of both sexes, the women clad in their gala costumes, assembled round the pyre. In a short time after their arrival, the fated victim appeared, accompanied by the Brahmins, her relatives, and the body of the deceased. The spectators showered chaplets of mogree on her head, and greeted her appearance with laudatory exclamations at her constancy and virtue. The women especially pressed forward to touch her garments; an act which is considered meritorious, and highly desirable for absolution, and protection from the Evil Eye.

The widow was a remarkably handsome woman, apparently about thirty, and most superbly attired. Her manner was marked by great apathy to all around her, and by a complete indifference to the preparations which for the first time met her eye: from this circumstance an impression was given that she might be under the influence of opium; and in conformity with the declared intention of the Europeàn officers present to interfere, should any coercive measures be adopted by the Brahmins, or relatives, two medical officers were requested to give their opinion on the subject. They both agreed that she was quite free from any influence calculated to induce torpor or intoxication.

Captain Burnes* then addressed the woman, desiring to know whether the act she was about to perform were voluntary, or enforced; and assuring her that, should she entertain the slightest reluctance to the fulfilment of her vow, he, on the part of the British government, would guaranty the pro-

* Then assistant resident in Cutch.

tection of her life and property. Her answer was calm, heroic, and constant to her purpose: "I die of my own free will; give me back my husband, and I will consent to live; if I die not with him, the souls of seven husbands will condemn me."* Having said this with a placid manner, which nothing appeared likely to change, further expostulation was deemed useless; but, as a message had been despatched to the Rao,† requesting his interference, an hour's delay was demanded. It was also insisted, that the crowd should withdraw to a short distance from the spot, leaving the widow alone with her relations; and the hope was great, that during this pause from the exciting influences of the scene, the tenderness of her nature might shake her resolution at the approach of death, and yet avail to save her. Before the full expiration of the hour, the Rao returned a message, declaring the inefficiency

* This woman declared that she had already passed seven times through the fire; having been Sadhwee for seven husbands; and should she now withdraw, they would rise and condemn her, according to the doctrine of the Shastrus, which says,—"As long as a woman shall decline burning herself, like a faithful wife, on the same fire as her deceased lord, so long shall she not be exempted from springing to life, in the body of some female animal." (Ungira.)

† The Rao's regard for the deceased had been very great, and in speaking of him as his friend, he gave him the poetical title of "his heart of hearts."

of his power to arrest the ceremony. Ere the renewal of the horrid ceremonies of death were permitted, again the voice of mercy, of expostulation, and even of entreaty, was heard; but the trial was vain, and the cool and collected manner with which the woman still declared her determination unalterable, chilled and startled the most courageous. Physical pangs evidently excited no fears in her: her singular creed, the customs of her country, and her sense of conjugal duty, excluded from her mind the natural emotions of personal dread; and never did martyr to a true cause go to the stake with more constancy and firmness, than did this delicate and gentle woman prepare to become the victim of a deliberate sacrifice to the demoniacal tenets of her heathen creed.

All further interference being useless, the ceremony proceeded. Accompanied by the officiating Brahmin, the widow walked seven times round the pyre, repeating the usual mantras, or prayers, strewing rice and coories* on the ground, and sprinkling water from her hand over the bystanders, who believe this to be efficacious in preventing disease and in expiating committed sins.† She then removed her jewels, and presented them to her relations, saying a few words to each, with a

* The current coin of Cutch.

† See Ward on the Hindus.

calm soft smile of encouragement and hope. The Brahmins then presented her with a lighted torch, bearing which,

> "Fresh as a flower just blown,
> And warm with life, her youthful pulses playing,"

she stepped through the fatal door, and sat within the pile. The body of her husband, wrapped in rich kinkaub, was then carried seven times round the pile, and finally laid across her knees. Thorns and grass were piled over the door; and again it was insisted, that free space should be left, as it was hoped the poor victim might yet relent, and rush from her fiery prison to the protection so freely offered. The command was readily obeyed, the strength of a child would have sufficed to burst the frail barrier which confined her, and a breathless pause succeeded; but the woman's constancy was faithful to the last; not a sigh broke the death-like silence of the crowd, until a slight smoke, curling from the summit of the pyre, and then a tongue of flame darting with bright and lightning-like rapidity into the clear blue sky, told us that the sacrifice was completed. Fearlessly had this courageous woman fired the pile, and not a groan had betrayed to us the moment when her spirit fled. At sight of the flame, a fiendish shout of exultation rent the air; the tom-toms sounded, the people clapped their hands with delight, as the evidence of their murderous work burst on their view; whilst the English spectators of this sad scene withdrew, bearing deep compassion in their hearts, to philosophise as best they might, on a custom so fraught with horror, so incompatible with reason, and so revolting to human sympathy.

The pile continued to burn for three hours; but, from its form, it is supposed that almost immediate suffocation must have terminated the sufferings of the unhappy victim. In producing this effect, the arrangement of the pyre I have described is far more merciful than that commonly used, which is a mere frame of bamboos covered with combustible matter, in the form of a bed, on which the bodies are laid, the quick and the dead bound together in a last embrace.

As some excuse for the infliction of horrible suffering on their fellow-creatures, with the power and inclination for which such a sacrifice seems to endue the natives of India, it is only just to remark, that the extent of their religious superstition leads these unhappy people to believe that no real physical agony is endured on occasions of this kind. In proof of this assertion, it may be mentioned, that on my speaking to an intelligent Hindu on the subject of this particular Suttee, he assured me that the woman had, previously to the ceremony, cooked some rice and milk together, with certain mantras and formulas; after which, by dipping her hand into the preparation, she was rendered callous to the flames. Moreover, that the soul of a woman, who is really Sadhwee,* departs to the paradise of Indra at the moment she fires the pile. By promulgating such absurdities as these, do the Brahmins of India impose on the darkened minds of an ignorant people, and uphold the performance of the most diabolical rites; subtlely hardening the hearts of their believers to the tears and prayers of the afflicted, to the dying shrieks of the widow, and the murder of the helpless; turning the hand of the Rajpoot father against his firstborn, and the arm of the son against his mother, and thus securing to themselves the unbridled enjoyment of power, wealth, and soul-debasing sensuality, to an extent too fearful to describe.

On passing the site of the pyre, some hours afterwards, all traces of the frame-work had disappeared; but on the ground which it had occupied were three chattees† containing balls of rice, which are usually placed by the son, or nearest relation, as an offering to the gods, where a body has been burned.

By order of the Rao, a tomb has since been erected on the spot. It is usual in all parts of Cutch to set up a large block of stone where a

* Pure.

† Earthen pots.

Suttee has been performed, and an upright hand and arm are carved on them as the emblem, and daubed with a pigment of red ochre.* The Rao's conduct in this matter is considered highly blameable, as notwithstanding the superstitions of his people, and the strong feeling of caste which connects itself in their minds with this time-consecrated sacrifice, his Highness's command would have sufficed to prevent it. There is, however, reason to fear, that his Highness, debased as his otherwise amiable character is by the tenets of Hinduism, secretly favoured and approved the Brahmins' proceedings; and so determined were the parties concerned not to admit a chance of our interference, until their arrangements were far advanced, that the intention of celebrating the funeral obsequies of Bhoojray was absolutely unknown to the British Resident, until their preparations for the tragedy were completed. The whole of the Rao's people were present, from his prime minister to the lowest wrestler of his court; and

* These stones are called Palliahs, and are peculiar to this province. Stones bearing various emblems also mark the place of a foray. They express in fact a violent death. When the Mahomedans first came to Cutch, and saw these Palliahs, bearing effigies, which are not permitted by their religion, they overthrew and destroyed them; on seeing which, the Hindus exchanged their emblems for the simple carving of a tree, which was not equally offensive. Several of these indications remain in the eastern part of the province.

this, at least, seemed like the tacit countenance of a deed, which, on his inauguration, he had pledged himself to use his highest influence to prevent.

The Bombay Government have expressed their disapprobation on the subject, and have notified to his Highness, that a repetition of the act will not be overlooked; it is hoped therefore, that Cutch will not be made the theatre of another scene, so full of horror, and which, even at a distance of time, it is impossible for the imagination to recal, without feelings of mingled compassion and disgust; disgust which not even the purest benevolence can allay.

Some time after this sacrifice, another was offered of a somewhat different character:* the beautiful mother of the Rao suddenly died from a violent attack of fever; one of her female attendants, a poor water-carrier, stated her intention to bury herself alive, in order that she should be in readiness to attend her beloved mistress in another state. Self-inhumation is not an uncommon means by which, as a work of extraordinary merit, the Hindus hope to testify at once their love for the deceased, and their right to great rewards in a future state. The Hindu is taught by his Puranas firmly to believe in the doctrine of a transmigration of souls, and that

* Written some time after I had the pleasure of visiting the harem.

after a short space of expiation in the realms of Yumu,* he will again arise in this world in a new, and probably a human birth.

This popular superstition, combined with the notion that through merit the individual who performs a self-sacrifice is at once released from the pangs of death, with only the appearance of suffering from the means used to destroy life, enlightens us with respect to what, under a different regulation of mind, seems irreconcilable with our ideas of human weakness, and the powerful instinct noticeable in civilized beings, to preserve life for its own sake; even though the sufferer who bears its privileges be contemned, friendless, or borne down with age and sickness, or those carking cares which would seem to make the days of the years of his life a sore burthen, little to be desired: he still cleaves to it, as his dearest treasure, still struggles to the last, to invigorate its flickering ray.

The Ranee's old water-bearer was doubtless supported by the opinions of her caste; and being oppressed by age, and many infirmities, she believed that they, being all inseparably connected with a former birth, might be laid down with her life, and that she might be born again to the enjoyment of energy, youth, and hope. In this case also, every persuasion was used to induce the devoted one to

* The Holy King who judges the dead.—Ward.

abandon her design; but of course ineffectually, and the poor old creature, having had a hole dug in the ground, near the large tomb, capable of holding her in a perpendicular position, suffered her son to lift her into it, and pile the earth about her. Before her grave was closed, while yet the breath of heaven fanned her face, and the glad scenes of life floated before her eyes, she made a request so singular, that I can find no one to account for it. She desired an inverted chattee to be placed over her head; which done, the earth was thrown over it, and in a few seconds trampled down with shouts of exultation. The unexhausted air in the chattee, must have preserved life for a short time after the grave had been filled in, and probably, while her pulse yet beat, the fiendish shouts of her murderers rang in her ears, and mingled with the agonizing death of this infatuated woman.

I have before observed, that self-sacrifice has been benevolently forbidden, in provinces which are under the British control, and is, therefore, less common on this side of India, than in Bengal. However, as the people have the power of travelling to those places which are still governed by native princes, the most zealous amongst them adopt this means of gratifying their wishes. I remember, while at Mandavie, once having seen three women arrive, after a seventeen days' voyage from Bombay, for the purpose of performing Suttee; and under peculiar circumstances, they are permitted to do so, without the presence of the husband's body: according to the Puranas, "if the husband die on a journey, or in a distant country, the widow, holding his sandals to her breast, may pass into the flames." One of these women had come to perform Suttee for her son, whom she stated to have been her husband in a former birth. This woman, who was advanced in years, went by on an open cart, triumphantly bearing a branch of the sacred Tulsi,* and surrounded by almost the whole population of Mandavie. I was not present at the ceremony, which took place at a distance of ten miles; but was afterwards assured, that the three widows became Sadhwee, with unshaken fortitude. According to strict Hinduism, in all cases of intended Suttee, an alternative is allowed; but it includes so many penances, so much self-mortification, and life becomes so complete a state of pain and privation, that it is hardly a matter of surprise, with the

* Ocymum or sweet basil. This plant has a dusky hue approaching to black, and thenee, perhaps, like the large black bee of this country, is held sacred to Krishna; though a fable perfectly Ovidian is told in the Puranas concerning the metamorphosis of the nymph Tulasi, who was beloved by the pastoral god, into the shrub which has since borne her name. —Asiatic Researches, vol. iv.

peculiar creed of the people, that the offer of life is seldom accepted; more particularly, as the Hindoo legislators evidently encourage this self-sacrifice of their widows. The policy of the Brahmins induces them to advocate it, as a work of supreme merit, and invest its ceremonial with all the brilliant *éclat*, which the presence of admiring and laudatory multitudes can bestow.

CHAPTER VII.

ANJAR.

Situation of the Town of Anjar.—British Residency.—Establishment of Rats.—Sacred Fish.—Vishnoo's First Avatara.—Legend of Jaisur Peer.—Domestic Habits of the Poor.—Precocity.—Wandering Fakirs.—Remarkable Brahmin Mendicant.—Population of Anjar.—Destructive Earthquake of 1819.—Legend of a Rishi, one of the Seven Holy Penitents.—Geological Character of Cutch.—Natural Convulsions of Earlier Periods.—Hindu Opinions respecting the Great Earthquake.

THE province of Cutch contains few towns of any commercial, or historical interest; and amongst these, Mandavie and Anjar alone deserve record. The palmy days of the latter have passed, but the town is still good, and its situation and neighbourhood are the most desirable in the province. Planted on a gracefully sloping elevation, near an extensive tank, it is surrounded by a wall forty feet high, with thirty-one strongly built towers. It is, in consequence, capable of being well fortified. The town of Anjar is situated in the most fertile part of Cutch; the neighbourhood abounds in game, and, the tank being well stocked with good fish, it is a favourite resort of the

Bhoojites, during what is called "the break in the rains," or the fair weather period, which usually intervenes between the early and the latter rain. Anjar was originally chosen as the seat of the British Government, and the Residency still remains in good order. It is commodious and well built, consisting of an upper and lower suite of rooms. The upper apartments are surrounded by a spacious verandah, which commands a fine view of the richly wooded country; the lower rooms are fantastically painted in the native taste, with gorgeous delineations of tigers, elephants, and various grotesque figures. Near the gates of the Residency is a Hindu temple, supposed, at one period, to have sheltered five thousand rats, *bonâ fide* rats, who were under the care of an old Gosein * of the establishment, whose custom it was to summon them all three times a-day, by means of a little bell, to a repast of grain scattered for their use on the floor of the temple. The poor old caterer has since passed away, and the rats have probably followed his example, as fifty only are now on the charitable fund.

The Hindus consider the preservation of all animals to be a work of peculiar merit; and though the truth of many anecdotes, once related of the animal hospital at Surat, is now doubted, there is no doubt of the existence of this boarding

* Religious devotee.

house for rats. Near another temple adjacent to the large tank, is a smaller one filled with fish, which I have seen regularly fed by the Brahmins with bread; the finny mendicants rising duly expectant to the surface at the appointed time. By the Hindus, fish are regarded as fit objects of worship; it being a point of belief with them, that Vishnoo, on his first avatara,* chose the form of a fish in which to become incarnate.

Connected with both these temples are several legends, but so essentially partaking of the character of old women's tales, that they are scarcely deserving of notice. From one of the traditions it would appear, that the creed of Islam, ungallant as its tenets are, allows the notion that a husband may become sanctified by the righteousness of his wife. The people of Anjar have a tale of one Jaisur Peer, a Mahomedan outlaw and robber, who married a beautiful Ranee named Tooree Kateranee, whose saintly virtues so won on the heart of her roguish and wicked husband, that he became converted to the highest reverence for religious mysteries. After death, Jaisur Peer and his wife were buried apart, though near each other; but the tombs are gradually approaching, (as is evident to the eyes of all true believers,) and at their meeting, the world will be no more.

* "Matya-avatara," or transformation into a fish.—See DUBOIS's *India*.

The Residency of Anjar is situated in the highest part of the town, and commands a general and unobstructed view. Without reference to the fine clumps of rich tamarind trees, which clothe the grassy slopes beyond the walls, the town itself appears thickly wooded: every little court yard is graced by a luxuriant tree, which throws up its kindly branches, and overshadows the poor inmates, as they sleep or spin during the noontide heat. Many of these trees are sacred, and are in consequence decorated with little white, blue, or red flags.

It is interesting to observe the domestic habits of these poor people, as the elevated position of the residency allows a stranger to do; and much more kindness, more activity, and purposeness, (if the term may be allowed) are observable, than, from our common opportunities of judging, we might readily believe could exist. It is usual for the families of two or three generations to reside in the same dwelling, which is frequently a better sort of shed, containing two or three bedsteads, some earthen vessels, and half a dozen rude spinning-wheels, which afford to the women and children their employment. The aged and widowed crone, slowly twirling the cotton with her trembling hand, the blooming matron, and the smiling child, may here constantly be seen labouring in the same monotonous vocation.

In addition to the numerous members of the family, the little court-yards are tenanted by cows and calves, which claim shelter there, and seem immediately under the authority of the younger branches of the family, who appear fully competent to the task assigned them. It is amusing to watch a little naked urchin, whose embryo strength is scarcely yet sufficiently developed to give his frame a steady gait, wield a long stick between his little hands, and, by a succession of tiny efforts, succeed in expelling some horned intruder.

In all countries the children of the poor are precocious, but remarkably so in the East, where the climate allows of their constant exposure, and where, as soon as they can walk, their services are required in behalf of domestic cares. Native children display a degree of shrewdness at an early age which seems to pass away as they advance in life, and forms no part of their character, as adults.

These court-yards also constitute places of call for innumerable wandering Fakirs, who extort the largess of a handful of grain, from the superstition of those who perhaps have but little to give ; and in return they bestow a benediction on the donors. Amongst a large fraternity of these mendicants, one individual is most remarkable. He is a spare, active, old Brahmin, who has been dumb from infancy, and gains a living, which would be but precarious in a civilized country, by his reputation for holiness. When I first observed him, he was receiving grain in a little copper vessel, from the pitiful store of a poverty-stricken and palsied old woman surrounded by a troop of naked and laughing grandchildren, to whom he was mowing and pointing with a vain attempt at articulation. In return for his grain, he fastened a small yellow thread round the woman's wrist, as a preservative against the Evil Eye. His cummerbund was filled with similar fragments of like salutary effect; and his neck, arms, and chest, were burthened by immense balls made from the wood of the Tulsi, and other sacred trees, and strung into necklaces and bracelets. These he bestowed more sparingly, and I believe made them an article of trifling barter.

This man had none of the characteristic indolence of his tribe: his loss of speech seemed to have greatly sharpened his remaining faculties, all of which were the ministers of the most engrossing selfishness. Even when the long cloth which he wore over his shoulders was wholly knotted into little bundles of grain, he still continued to run rapidly from house to house, with the speed of a squirrel, stopping for a moment, as he received his largess, then darting away to a second threshold, and at the same moment, holding up his hand to the owner of a third, to signify his immediate attendance; begging at the same time, from the passers by, a portion of whatever they might be carrying, a bit of betel, or cocoa-nut, a fragment of water-melon, or a few vegetables. Nothing escaped him; and as he darted about, appropriating every thing he could possibly seize, and stuffing it hastily into his wallet, he reminded one, Brahmin as he was, more of a clown in a pantomime than of the dignitary of a religious order.

Some idea of the flourishing state of mendicity in a small native town may be gained from the fact, that at Anjar, in addition to thirteen castes of Brahmins, who all subsist on public contributions, there are no fewer than one hundred and forty religious mendicants.

The population of the town is principally Hindu, of whom there are forty-two different castes, each caste, as is usual, carrying on a distinct and hereditary calling. Amongst them may be found, potters, dyers, workers in metal, oil-expressers, basket-makers, barbers, story-tellers, and weavers. Brahmins, and Banyans, abound every where.

Anjar seems originally to have been a village of inconsiderable size; but it was much enlarged and improved immediately before, and also since the calamity of an earthquake, whose effects are strongly evidenced in Cutch. Of this fact we are informed, by a curious Guzzerati inscription, near each of the five gates of the city. Of this the following is a translation:—

"After worship to Guneesa and Ashápurá, then be honour to Hujeepál and Mahadeo-raee.

"In the year of Vicram, 1875, in the month Jét,* on the ninth of the dark half, an earthquake happened, at which time the fort of Anjar was destroyed; but during the minority of the illustrious Maharaj Rao Daisuljee, the regency ordered its re-erection; and in the beginning of the month Assar,† in the year of Vicram, 1882, the work was commenced, the subjects were made happy, and the city was rendered flourishing. At that time, Ambaram Rajaram, of the village of Arnhar, was Kamdar,‡ and superintended the work, the head workman being Jugnaal Peetamber."

EARTHQUAKE OF 1819.

The walls and towers of Anjar suffered materially from this earthquake, by which also much damage was caused throughout the province. The convulsion seems to have been felt all over India, but its severity was greater in Cutch than in the neighbouring provinces. One thousand

* Jét (or June.) † Assar (or July).

‡ The town collector and magistrate.

five hundred houses were destroyed in Anjar, and about two hundred lives lost. Bhooj, however, appears to have been most severely visited by this calamity: nearly seven thousand houses were destroyed, and not fewer than eleven hundred and fifty people buried in the ruins. To increase the confusion, the royal elephants broke from their pickets, and rushed through the city, spreading terror around, and causing incalculable mischief, until stopped in their career by the falling houses. The natives, during this confusion, were terrified at the pheuomenon, in proportion to their inability to account for it ; and it is deserving of remark, that they all seem to have been conscious of a sense of giddiness and sickness before experiencing the severe shock.

It is remarkable that, although the appearance of Cutch is peculiarly volcanic, consisting of chains of irregular rusty-looking hills,* covered with fragments of half detached rocks, yet the natives never blend the tradition of a previous earthquake with any of their legends. They say, that a very holy man, a Rishi,† who had been long dwelling on the banks of a river in Cutch, absorbed in

* Probably containing much sulphuret of iron, as sulphur in a pure state has been found in Cutch.

† The Rishis were seven holy penitents, who were translated to the celestial regions, and now form the constellation of Ursa Major.

meditation, determined to render this barren land fruitful; he therefore subjected it by his power to the influence of fire: flames burst forth over the land; and, having devastated and destroyed all on its surface, the fire was succeeded by fertility, calm waters, and green pasture, attracting to it the pastoral tribes of neighbouring provinces.*

The appearance of the country is in accordance with this cunningly devised fable: the hills seem but recently to have emerged from a state of fusion; the masses of rock are black and bare, thrown together in wild and chaotic forms, and in many parts torn and rent asunder, presenting large chasms, down which, during the monsoon, rapid torrents sweep with resistless force into the plains, irrigating the valleys, which become covered with a stunted brushwood, affording good pasture for numerous herds of sheep and goats. This, however, fails with the rains, and a soft sandy soil is again the principal feature of this sterile land. From its general appearance, its natural productions,† and the present state of its ruins, it is to be inferred that Cutch has at various times suffered from similar natural convulsions, which, however,

* See Captain Macmurdo's paper in the Bombay Literary Transactions, vol. i.

† Specimens of iron ore are every where abundant; sulphur has been found; and saltpetre is made in large quantities from the soil.

are not on record. Great alarm appears to have been caused by the remarkable circumstances attending this earthquake: in one part of the province, the earth suddenly opened, and water issued from the cavity; several dry beds of rivers became filled with water which resembled blood, from the soil through which it had been forced; and about Anjar, the water in the wells assumed a milky appearance.

During the first great shock, which occupied about two minutes, the town of Bhooj became nearly a heap of ruins; and from east to west, did the angel of destruction sweep over this devoted province: from Wagur to Luckput on the Indus, all the stones of the villages were levelled with the dust, and all the towns and forts were materially injured.

The Hindus purified themselves, and made offerings to appease the wrath of the terrible Siva.* The Mahomedan Moolahs† stated the cause of the earthquake to be the horse Dooldool, pawing for his food. Thus, in the midst of terror and consternation, human selfishness prevailed: the Brahmins exhorted the people to make liberal donations to their temples, as a means of evading the destroyer's arm; and the Moolahs enjoined

* Siva, the destroyer, the third person of the Hindu Trinity.

† Priests.

their disciples to send grain to satisfy the good steed, Dooldool, whose supplies were appropriated to the private use of the pious priests of the prophet. All sorts and varieties of ludicrous stories were framed for the explanation of this great phenomenon; and the more absurd, the more readily were they believed. It appears that in the same year, great convulsions were experienced at Etna and at Vesuvius, and earthquakes were felt in many parts of Italy. It may be worthy of remark, that the prickly pear tree, which grows in such luxuriance amongst the lava on the sides of mount Etna, also flourishes abundantly in Cutch. The superior growth of the vine, in the neighbourhood of mount Etna, is there accounted for by the rich manure of the prickly pear, when in a state of decomposition; and it is curious, that Cutch also is celebrated for the fineness of its grapes.

Previously to this earthquake, whose effects produced such ruin in this particular province, several shocks had been felt in other parts of India. The natives must, in consequence, have begun to think the world was fearfully increasing in sin; as the favourite Hindu tenet connected with the subject is, that the world is supported by an enormous, many-headed snake; that only one head sustains it at a time; and that, as the snake becomes fatigued, he slips it off upon another, which produces a corresponding effect of motion on the surface of the globe, occasioning earthquakes of greater or less force, according to the weight of the earth, and the effort the snake makes to change its position. Now, say these ingenious theorists, the earth becomes heavy in proportion to the sins of men; and as crime increases, the supporting head of the snake becomes more frequently fatigued, and earthquakes of course more frequent.

In this way does the Hindu philosopher satisfy himself, by referring the operations of nature to the causes assigned by monstrous and absurd fables, ingenious in their construction, and consistent, according to their system of parts. Thus, if you ask him, how this snake is supported, he at once tells you, it is on the sure foundation of the back of a huge tortoise; and if you inquire, to what the tortoise is indebted, for being so sustained under its double load, his answer is ready — "by the power of Brahma." This first cause, however, would not have satisfied the Hindu's imagination, without the secondary agents of the tortoise, and the snake: the simplicity of nature was above the level of his understanding.

CHAPTER VIII.

THE RUNN.

Extent and Locality of the Great Northern Runn. — Mirage. — Islands on the Runn.—Hindu Apollo.—Indian Pastorals.—Zoology of the Runn. — Hog-hunting. — Indian Sports, Poetry, and Music. — The Wild Ass.—Black Partridge.—Sacred Birds.—Paroquets.

THROUGHOUT Western India, nothing could, perhaps, be found more worthy the observation of the traveller, than the great northern Runn; a desert salt plain, which bounds Cutch on the north and east, and extends from the western confines of Guzzerat to the eastern branch of the river Indus; approaching Bhooj at its nearest point, at about the distance of sixteen miles. This tract is of large extent, and between the months of May and October is flooded with salt water. During other parts of the year it is passable; but the glare is so great from the incrustation of salt, caused by the evaporation of the water, that it is seldom attempted, unless from the inducements of trade, or the necessities of military duty.

The distant aspect of the Runn resembles that of the ocean at ebb tide; and as some water always remains on it, the refraction of light produces the most beautiful and mysterious effects, decorating it with all the enchantments of the most lovely specimens of mirage, whose magic power, exerting itself on the morning mists, indues this desert tract with the most bewitching scenes: rock, and hill, and tower; palmy hillocks, clumps of rich foliage, turreted castles, and gothic arches, alike appear in quick succession, to charm and beguile the traveller; and

> "The wayworn spirit hath a gleam
> Of sunny vales and woods;"

until, again slowly dissolving in the thin ether from which their fantastic forms emerged, they cheat him with their fair delusions, and pass away like a dream of fairy land.

There are several islands on the Runn, and a bright oasis of grassy land, known by the unromantic name of the Bunni. Thither, in patriarchal style, the shepherds take their flocks, and lead a sunny pastoral life, although surrounded by a desert marsh. An acquaintance with the shepherds' life of India may illustrate some of the beautiful allegories of the inspired writings; but it excites no desire to share the pleasure of those happy swains, whose

> "Rural pleasures crown their happiness."

True, the Hindu writers describe their Apollo,* in the full enjoyment of a pastoral scene, worthy the birthplace of the Georgics; but the stern realities of Indian shepherdism form a woeful bathos to all this. It is compounded of dirt, weariness, and apparently never-ending toil: a poor being, the Damon of a filthy village, with stick in hand, and just such covering rags as a satirist might call clothes, sets out at day-break, in charge of, perhaps, sixty cows, and as many goats, to drive them to the hills for pasture. There he remains, solitary, ignorant, and dinnerless until sunset, when he returns with his charge, half suffocated and spiritless, to find solace in his chillum, and rest, under his dirty blanket, in the corner of a miserable shed.

Not always, however, does this poor animal machine alone attend his daily care. Sometimes, on a burning afternoon, when the weary kine lag slowly homeward, a woman may be seen, a gentle Phyllis with bare legs, bare feet, her coarse black hair streaming wildly from her face, as with a huge branch of some hastily plundered tree in her hand, she urges on the cattle, utterly regardless of thorns and brambles, as she loudly vociferates to her charge. The logical Master Touchstone would hardly be sceptical as to the character of such a shepherd's life as this; he would declare at

* Krishna.

once, "that in respect it is a shepherd's life, it is a very vile life." So much for Indian pastorals: it is a true sketch, but not particularly illustrative of life on the Bunni, which tract, being remarkably fertile, has unusual advantages for the ruminating species. I speak of the pastoral life as it is generally found in India; readers being too often misled, by having only one feature of a country, a mere isolated fact presented to them, from which they form a general, and of course, an erroneous opinion. Delusion is abroad; tourists write, and artists paint, heedless of fact; anxious only to bathe a favourite spot in all the light of graceful beauty, and the bright hues their own glowing and poetic imaginations suggest. But surely, if it be once admitted that truth alone is the keystone of knowledge, and consequently the only associate of good taste, it were better, where facts really exist, that ornament should be deemed superfluous and ill placed; and I have no doubt that, as real knowledge increases, its vanities will be seen, and the simple and vivid delineation of truth be held in most esteem, and constitute the real triumph of literature and the fine arts. Teniers will find more admirers than Nicholas Poussin, and those writers gather greatest fame, who

> "Pour out all as plain
> As downright Shippen, or as old Montaigne."

Then will nature be worshipped as she alone deserves, divested of the meretricious garb which only veils her beauty; she will be sought for by the path of knowledge, science will be the ministering flamen of her mysteries, and the many will feel the harmony of her simple beauty. The institutions of man will be purified by her influence, his mind will recognise its powers, facts will appear, opinions will change, systems will arise, sincerity and benevolence will radiate throughout the world; and, reaching even the palmy shores of India, may plead the cause of the poor Hindu within the heart of man, and prove,

> "That where Britain's pow'r
> Is felt, mankind will feel her mercy too."

The Runn abounds with wild animals; and the wolf, the boar, and the wild ass claim it for their dwelling-place. The borders of the Runn, being rocky and precipitous, afford them perfect protection; and the vegetation on the marshy ground near the Bunni, and in other parts, affords them excellent pasture. It would not be uninteresting to a zoologist to cross this singular tract. Independently of the peculiar and rare character of its soil and general appearance, the natives have a custom of gathering together the whitened bones of the animals they find on it, with which they mark the road, to guide the traveller during either night or day.

The "grim grey boar" of the Indian jungle is too well known to require description, and the spirit-stirring sport his chase affords has long employed the pen of the sportsman and the poet, in its praise. Cutch has ever been noted amongst the brethren of the spear, for its abundance of game; and in the fastnesses of its rocky hills, lurk the grimmest monsters of the foamy tusk, ever ready,

> "To lead the throng of the chase along
> With their spears all dashed with gore,
> And try the speed of the fleetest steed,
> Who ne'er was tried before."

Indian sports have lost a noble recorder in the author of these lines,* as well as many other exhilarating melodies, descriptive of the noble sport of hog-hunting. The spirit of poetry no longer sheds the halo of genius round the spear; but the enthusiasm amongst its votaries remains, and the wise and brave are still lured to the jungle side; and when the cares and the toils of the chase are o'er, and the brimming cup goes round, the full choruses of these noble songs restore to them the raptures of the day.

The most remarkable animal on this vast tract is the wild ass. It is singularly marked, and

* Major Morris.

stands about thirteen hands high. It is of a light fawn colour, with a broad dun stripe down the middle of the back, and is handsome and well shaped. Herodotus tells us, that the Medes used wild asses to draw their chariots of war;* but it is difficult to imagine the animal controlled sufficiently for this purpose, as its nature seems peculiarly wild and untameable, and its fleetness enables it to distance the boldest riders. We had one captured on the Runn by means of a lasso, when very young: it was of small size, and a playful pretty little creature — a sort of pet in our camp, where it was suffered to trot about as it liked, never having betrayed any desire to return to its native wilds. In this case civilization had been active, for the character of the animal is undeniably timid. However, as no one has ever succeeded in capturing one of the species, when full grown, it is impossible to judge what degree of docility it might acquire, by a long domestication with man; but I am induced to believe, that the nature of the wild ass is still the same as it was in the land of Uz, when Job cried, — "Who hath sent out the wild ass free? or who hath loosed the bands of the wild ass? whose house I have made the wilderness, and the barren land his dwelling. He scorneth the multitude of the city, neither re-

* See Book vii.

gardeth he the crying of the driver. The range of the mountains is his pasture, and he searcheth after every green thing."*

The wild ass is peculiar to the Runn; but, perhaps, no given spot of a similar size is so rife with animal existence as the whole province of Cutch, which literally abounds with game. Amongst the various species, is a rare and very beautiful bird, known as the black partridge, but differing materially from the bird so called in other parts of India. The breast of the male bird is covered with jet-black feathers, with a spot of clear white on each feather; over the eye, which is remarkably brilliant, is a red stripe, and below it, a line of white feathers; the feathers of the wings are of a bright brown, and a ring of the same coloured plumage encircles the throat. This partridge has a shrill and peculiar cry, which may be heard at a considerable distance. As a delicacy for the table, it is highly esteemed.

There is also an abundant supply of the more general description of game; bustard, quail, cullum, hares, pea-fowl, and wild duck of many varieties, from the teal, to the fine grey duck so well known. It is well stocked, too, with animals of the ferine order; jackals, wolves, hyenas, foxes, and bats, (according to the classification of M. Cuvier,) whilst during the rainy season, the

* Book of Job, chap. xxxix.

tanks are visited by numerous birds of the wader class, flamingoes, spoonbills, pelicans, &c.

The natives never destroy these animals, and their number is in consequence large. In common with the ancient Greeks, the Hindus hold the peafowl sacred; and the plantations are thickly tenanted by these beautiful birds, which strut about, displaying their gorgeous plumage in full assurance of security. Paroquets are also held in reverence, the people believing that they are indebted to them for the origin of their fruits and flowers, the seeds of which, they say, the paroquets brought from the gardens of Paradise, and dropped upon the earth.

CHAPTER IX.

RELIGIOUS CEREMONIES IN CUTCH.

THE NAGA PACHAMI.

Holy Processions.—The Hooli.—Worship of the Naga Pachami, or Cobra Capella.—Ceremonies of Snake Worship.—Presence and Participation of the Rao.—Legend of Sirdaee; or, the Origin of Snake Worship.—Reflections on the Worship of Idols.—Bigotry of the Hindus.—Policy of the British Government.

"This day to Dagon is a solemn feast,
With sacrifices, triumphs, pomps, and games."
Samson Agonistes.

THE procession of the ornamented bier of the sons of Ali, known as the Taibout, which takes place during the Mahomedan fast of the Mohurrum, throughout India, has been too frequently described to require further attention. In Cutch, however, the people, departing from the true spirit of the celebration, make it an occasion of rejoicing, in which Hindus as well as Mussulmans join, and appear in the procession, disguised as elephants, &c., creating boisterous mirth, and uncontrollable confusion.

The Hooli, a well known festival in honour of the goddess Doorga, is kept by the Hindus during the early part of spring, with the usual abandonment to idleness and licentiousness, which marks this celebration in all parts of India. The worship of the Naga Pachami, or Cobra Capella, may deserve notice from its peculiarity. It takes place annually, during what the natives call the light half of the month Srawun, corresponding with our August, and is attended by his Highness the Rao, the whole population of Bhooj and its vicinity, with many from afar, who come up to "Ramoth Gilead" to join in the worship.

The small temple dedicated to the Cobra is situated on the wall of the hill-fort of Bhoojeiah;* but its elevation and restricted dimensions rendering it peculiarly unsuited to the reception of a multitude, a temporary platform is erected below it, for the purposes of sacrifice. At the anniversary celebration, at which I was present, the ceremonies commenced at a very early hour; and before six o'clock, the platform, supporting a stone altar garlanded with flowers, and a guardi† for his Highness, was spread with rich carpets, and hung with a Kinkaub canopy; while from every part of the plain the eye commanded, horsemen might be seen, caracoling their anxious steeds,

* Before mentioned as the Snake Tower.

† A pile of cushions, considered as a throne.

or rapidly proceeding towards the place of rendezvous. It was about sunrise : the great globe of light had just glanced

> "Through the horizontal misty air,"

and illumined tree, and hill, and flower, with its radiant glow, when a long and gorgeous cavalcade emerged from the city gate, and soon came fully into view, advancing across the plain, towards the position we had taken.

In advance of the procession came the Rao's Sanees, or riding camels, richly caparisoned, bearing his standards and the Nekarah, or royal drum ; the drum being decorated with embroidered trappings, whose bright hues flashed like jewels in the morning sun. Next in order, with slow and stately pace, advanced the royal elephants, their faces and ears tattooed, circlets of pearl around their tusks, silver bells on their ankles, and bearing richly ornamented howdahs.

In the centre of the cavalcade appeared his Highness, surrounded by an immense concourse of horsemen mounted on gallant chargers, who chafed at the bit which restrained their impetuosity ; whilst other riders, of superior equestrian skill, suffered their steeds to break from the procession, and, after some graceful curvets, or careering them in a hand gallop for a few moments, fell again into their places, to swell the train of his Highness's followers. Altogether, their fine horses, decorated with silken and many-coloured trappings, their tall spears, graceful dress, and magnificently bossed shields, were admirably picturesque;—whilst

> "Bandrol, and scroll, and pennon there,
> O'er that procession flew:"—

and a sonorous strain of cymbals, tom-toms, and other native music, awakened the echoes, and murmuringly died away in the silent depths of the neighbouring hills.

His Highness was met at the foot of the hill by a party of Seapoys, and most of the European officers of the force; accompanied by whom he ascended to the platform, and was there received by the Brahmins. On his Highness's right hand, was seated his father, the ex-Rao Bharmuljee; a fine-looking man, apparently not more than forty years of age, but bearing in his countenance full evidence of his previous habits of intemperance and depravity.

The Brahmins, after repeating before the altar a variety of mantras to propitiate their Deity, led forward two goats, designed for sacrifice, and decorated with wreaths of mogree and chumpa. A few parched peas and a little bran were first laid on the altar, and then offered to the goats, who immediately ate them, in perfect confidence. This being received as a propitious augury, an attendant on the ceremonies bared a glittering scimitar, and, after whirling it in the air, at one descending blow severed the heads of the poor goats, which rolled bleeding towards the altar. Branches of the tulsi-tree were then dipped in the blood, and struck on the sides of the altar. The officiating priest, moistening a little red ochre with the blood, danced up to the Rao in a devout extasy, and affixed a circular mark with the pigment on his forehead: other mantras were then repeated; and the Brahmin, declaring the sacrifice accepted, immediately appeared to become possessed by a frenzy of excitement, dancing violently with all sorts of horrible gestures before the altar, flogging himself with a huge chain, and rolling on the ground, like a maniac. After this disgusting exhibition had continued for some time, his Highness left the scene, and returned, with the state already described, to his palace.*

* The Rao is in the frequent habit of visiting a small temple dedicated to Parvati, at the village of Rhoda, near Bhooj, thence called Rhoda Mata; Mata, signifying mother; and Parvati, under the various names of Bhowani, Ashapura, Devi, &c., is worshipped as a protecting goddess all over Cutch. At this place, the Rao sacrifices a buffalo, in the following manner: the animal is brought before the altar of the goddess, and a bundle of grass is thrown at its feet. As it stoops to eat, a few drops of water are scattered between its horns; and from the animal's gestures, as they trickle over its

In the absence of all historical record, on

"What shallow-searching Fame hath left untold,"

with respect to the origin of this singularly conducted worship, the natives have again recourse to an ingenious legend for explanation.

It is said, that in the olden time, there dwelt in the Puchum,* a passing fair, and very wealthy dame called Sirdaee, who possessed slaves in abundance, singing men and singing women, dancing girls, and all the usual attendants of Eastern pomp; and that this Sirdaee was, moreover, possessed of great learning, acquainted with the arts of divination, and a notable Sampuri.† Many Sampuries came daily to display to her their cunning; but the fair Sirdaee amused herself by working counter-charms against their art, by which means she became possessed of their snakes, and made the Sampuries her slaves.

forehead, auguries are drawn. If the creature shake its head, it is led away as displeasing to the goddess, and another of the herd is substituted; but, if it nod its head, the signal is sufficient, a glittering scimitar descends on its neck, another blow severs the sinews of the legs, and a third, aimed on the back, prostrates the dying beast. Mantras are then said, whilst the goddess is supposed to quaff its blood. Out-caste Hindus then drag the carcass from the sanctum; and, as they revel on its flesh, may be said to share the banquet of the propitiated goddess.

* An island on the Runn.

† Snake charmer.

The fame of this wonderful and beautiful woman becoming known, a young prince, himself a Sampuri, became enamoured of her description, and determined to see her. Sirdaee, by her power of foretelling events, became acquainted with his intentions, and, calling her handmaidens, instructed them to put on their rich attire, as a young and handsome prince was about to visit her, disguised as a Sampuri. At the time Sirdaee's knowledge led her to expect the prince, an old man, tottering and decrepit, with wrinkled countenance, blanched hair, and a silvery beard descending to his cummerbund,* craved admission, as a Sampuri, desiring to display his art to the noble lady of the palace.

The fair Sirdaee immediately knew him to be the disguised prince, and received him, brilliantly apparelled, and surrounded by her handmaidens. The pretended Sampuri challenged her to a trial of skill, which she accepted, and as usual surpassed the performances of her competitor. After his acknowledgment of the potency of her charm, however, she told him that although she had triumphed over many Sampuries, who with their snakes were now her slaves, one snake alone continued to defy her power. "Can you," said she, "but take him, all I have shall be yours, and I will even become your slave."

* Roll of cloth worn round the waist.

The young prince, enchanted at what seemed to promise such easy means of gaining power over so much wealth and beauty, eagerly pledged himself to obey her wishes; and the strong hold of the snake being pointed out to him, he at once set out on his mission.

Having arrived at the foot of a mountain, where the snake lay basking in the sun, he prepared to seize him; but the creature, raising itself in a menacing attitude, said, "Oh! foolish man, how canst thou hope to take me, who am possessed of greater power than all the Sampuri? Return and relinquish so vain a pursuit." But the prince replied, "Never! I will take you a prisoner to the beautiful Sirdaee, or perish in the attempt." On hearing this, the snake uncoiled its gigantic form, and rapidly left the mountain, followed by the prince; and thus they kept up the chase for months; the snake sometimes above the ground, and sometimes again, to elude the swiftness of his pursuer, disappearing, and travelling below it; and wherever the snake did so, rivers* sprang up, which may still be seen in Cutch.

It appeared that the prince possessed power in the proportion of twenty-five to twenty over the snake; but as often as the snake desired him to relinquish the pursuit, and he refused, a portion of this power departed, until the proportion be-

* Called Nagnics.

came in favour of the snake. Thus they journeyed, until the prince's power being greatly diminished, the snake attacked him, and bit him so that he died. But, before he did so, he called together the Sampuries who had gathered round him from curiosity as he travelled, and desired them, on his death, to burn his body, and devour the ashes, which would give them power over the snake to destroy it.

In odedience to this command, the Sampuries carried the body of the prince to the large hill of Bhoojeiah, and burnt it; but the snake had arrived there before them, and, alarmed at their preparation to eat the ashes, he assumed the form of a handsome young Brahmin, and standing amongst them inquired their purpose. After the Sampuries had told their story, he said, "Beware how you do this; for every one who even touches these ashes will become afflicted with leprosy." When they heard this, the Sampuries left the ashes, and dispersed, every man to his own home.

The snake then finding this hill a pleasant one, and not caring to return, made it his habitation. At a previous period, the Rao of Cutch, whose city lay at some distance, finding this delightful hunting ground, was in the habit of frequenting it, with the Jharrejah chiefs, and great men of the province; but from the time that the great Cobra arrived there, the animals became unusually ferocious, and the hares were seen to attack the dogs instead of fleeing from their pursuit. Moreover, snakes in great numbers came to Bhoojeiah; and at last the Rao, finding so fair and favourite a place becoming a desert region, ordered the people to clear the hill of Bhoojeiah, and build on it a strong fort. The workmen, endeavouring to obey the Rao's commands, were harassed by the attacks of the snakes and other animals which infested the hill, and many died. At length, a Megwah,* a wealthy man about the Rao, found the great Cobra, who told him, that his power should prevent all progress in the work, unless his dwelling were held sacred, and his power worshipped on Bhoojeiah. The Megwah pledged himself to observe these conditions. Accordingly, the fort was soon completed, and a small tower built over the dwelling, and dedicated to the worship of the Naga, or snake, as described. The festival is annually attended by the Rao of Cutch, accompanied by his chiefs and dependants.

The performance of the sacrifice is a privilege in the family of the Megwah. The present officiating priest, who is his blood descendant, receives a monthly stipend of coories, ghee, sugar, and grain; and, at the anniversary of the Naga Pachami, he is presented with new clothes and other largesses.

* Low-caste native.

Such is the legend connected with the snake-worship, which I received from an intelligent native well acquainted with the traditions of Cutch, and himself a Brahmin. It is curious from its ingenuity, and from the characteristic mode in which it is made to account for the worship of a reptile so pernicious to man as the Cobra Capella. Cutch abounds with these snakes during the rainy season; and I have no doubt, but the fear of so noxious a creature originally suggested the necessity of propitiating it as a Deity. It is interesting to trace the legendary lore of an unsophisticated and barbarous people to its source; and a philosophical inquiry into the origin of legends, combined with the histories of their ballads and war-songs, would, perhaps, throw a light on their early mental and physical state, more valuable than can be derived from any investigation of their unconnected and unauthenticated manuscript details of governments and conquests.

All the varied forms of idol worship, and the reverence shown during the early ages of the world to the objects of nature, must have found their source, less in the affections than in the fears of man, and in the necessity which he felt the weakness of his nature and constitution imposed on him, of seeking protection, against the many evils which surround him, from a superior power. The activity of his observation would lead him to invest the material objects of the visible world in which he moved with supposed powers, to the idea of which their habits, instincts, or beauty might give rise ; and his reflections on his mental faculties would lead him to form fanciful personifications of moral qualities, and reduce them to a tangible form. By degrees, the corruptions of the heart of man became the means by which the supposititious characters of these deities were deteriorated; for man, to countenance the desperate evils of his social character, found it necessary to indue his deities with the most violent and debasing passions, in order that he might worship them with such ceremonies, and propitiate them with such sacrifices, as might at once ensure him their protection, and suffer their worshipper to revel in the uninterrupted enjoyment of luxury and licentiousness. The warlike northern savage, delighting in blood, made the sacrifice of human victims the offering, by which his gods, Woden and Thor, were most readily propitiated ; the softer Greeks, revelling in gaiety and pleasure, cultivated the refined luxuries of civilized life, and worshipped music, poetry, and love, in the exquisitely chiselled forms of their tutelary deities ; while the Hindu, uninstructed and insensible, with passions heated as his clime, and careless of all but his animal nature and its provisions, makes unto himself a god, indues its supposed character with similar, but exaggerated passions to his own, and worships it with revolting and indecent orgies. He makes the richly sculptured temples of his deities, like his own heart, the theatre of all uncleanness, and the recorded history of their lives, a chronicle of the most absurd and impure legends. But,

> "High o'er the Eastern steep, the sun is beaming,
> And darkness flees with her deceitful shadows;
> So truth prevails o'er falsehood,"

and ere long it may so prevail, as to banish from the temples of Hinduism the monstrous personifications of depravity, which now fill them with a noxious darkness. What will be the means to effect this introduction of truth, is a moral problem yet to be solved; but "the history of the world is a history of progress;" and as it was beautifully remarked, that, as in the block of marble was a statue of exquisite form, which required only the chisel of the sculptor to bring it into light,* so does the spirit of truth exist in the least polished of nature's works, requiring only the aid of well adapted circumstances to remove the rubbish of prejudice and error which conceals it, and to lead it forth in the full brightness of its original beauty, to purify, irradiate, and convince.

The existing state of this bigoted people may

* Aristotle's doctrine of substantial forms.

appear to present unusual obstacles to moral improvement; but on inquiry into the past history of nations, the error of this opinion is easily traced. Can we doubt the capacity of the Hindus for improvement and civilization, when we remember the condition of England under the Scandinavian and Saxon rule, and that of its Druidical priesthood; and recall their sacrifices to Odin, little less horrible than the worship of Juggernath? Historical evidence proves, that the darkness of blood-stained idolatry has been again and again dissipated by civilization, and the people who lay under its yoke emancipated, and led by the way of knowledge to tolerance and patriotic virtue; and shall not the day-spring, then, visit the Hindu?

In most cases, the hand of the conqueror has scattered the seed of improvement, and civilization has followed the track of his chariot-wheel; but it must be remembered, that the love of liberty is twin-sister to the love of knowledge; and both will unfold themselves together, in the minds of those whom the introduction of truth may awaken to seek redress

"For India's injured realm."

Here rests the question; and it should be fairly investigated, without subterfuge, and without delay: Will our interests permit us to civilize the

Hindus? Shall India wear her plumed and jewelled turban with an air of peace? Or are her civil warfare, and her darkened policy, necessary to our wealth and safety? We are the conquerors, and in our power it rests. We know we cannot convert them to Christianity, as a people — we know we cannot throw down the barrier of castes — without *first* supplying them with intellectual and moral truth. Experience continues to teach us this, and reflection must convince us that her teaching is just. Can we then hope, that learning, and wisdom, change of opinion, and the conviction of power so gained, will attach these people to us by the social band of gratitude and reverence? or may we not rather fear, that the desire of liberty may rise so warmly in their hearts, that, once possessed of means adapted to such ends, they may spurn our control, trample on our government, and at length expel us from their rich and glowing land? It would be well to consider this: the riches of India, which first attracted us to her shores, are rapidly diminishing, from the want of knowledge, and of self-interest of sufficient power to stimulate the natives to industry. Her plains, rich and fertile as they might be made, lie desert and uncultivated; her mines are unworked, her manufactures unimproved; and where individual interest commands that the land should yield her increase, it is obtained only by a waste of human labour, grievous to behold. Such is the effect of the system we have long acted upon in India; but the present is not the time calculated to support its continuance. A new description of European society has lately been introduced to her capitals, and will rapidly increase, and spread over the country. Ere many years elapse, we shall have a middle and working class of Anglo-Indians; and from their examples, a power will be acquired by the native population, highly prejudicial to our interests, unless some means are taken to anticipate the effect of this supposed introduction of general, mechanical, and agricultural improvement. Thus, at this particular epoch in the history of our Indian possessions, the question of native improvement appears to carry with it considerations of very high political importance.

Our policy is liberal, our councils are founded on benevolence and justice, our native land yields to none in her energetic efforts to deliver the oppressed from him that is too strong for him, and to diffuse knowledge and tolerance amongst her people. Let, then, the conquered of her colonies share the influence of her civilizing power, that so wisdom, religion, and peace shall "circulate through every vein of all your empire;" or at least, let the question be entertained, if only on the ground of political security.

"Britain! thy voice can bid the dawn ascend!
On thee alone, the eye of Asia bend!
High arbitress! to thee her hopes are given,
Sole pledge of bliss, and delegate of Heaven.
In thy dark mantle all her fates repose,
Or bright with blessings, or o'ercast with woes;
And future ages shall thy mandate keep,
Smile at thy touch, or at thy bidding weep."*

* Mr. GRANT's Prize Poem, "*On the Restoration of Learning in the East.*"

CHAPTER X.

RELIGIOUS SECTS IN CUTCH.

Division of Sects. — Hinduism and Mahomedanism. — Benevolence of Hindus towards Brute Animals. — Sect of the Jains.—Singularity of Costume. —Religious Tenets. — Jain Temples. — Monastic Establishments.—Kanphuttees of Denodur.—Charitable Principles. — Celibacy. — Comparison of the Kanphuttees with the Monastic Orders of Europe.—Costume of Tournath, the Kanphuttee Peer, or Superior. — Derivation of the word Kanphuttee. — Fakirs of the Gosein.—Legend of Dhurrumnath.—Sect of the Kaprias of Mhurr. —Privileges of the Rajah of the Kaprias.—Idol Temple of Parvati. —Division of Hindu Cycles, or Ages.

In all countries where the supreme government has been at different times entrusted to princes professing a variety of religious faiths, the tenets of the people have undergone many breaches of unity, and a multiplicity of sects prevail. The crosier and the sceptre usually support each other; but party feeling, and not unfrequently political prejudice, originate schisms amongst the many, and their religious opinions form a parti-coloured tissue.

As in England the Catholic and Protestant creeds formed the great divisions in opinion and interests, in similar manner have Hinduism and Mahomedanism shared the religious enthusiasm of the Asiatics; but under both dispensations, minor pegs, on which to hang the garment of faith, have been introduced, either from a sentiment of benevolence, an idiosyncracy of mind, or such unworthy motives of self-distinction as are commonly mingled with novel systems for leading men to heaven.

In Cutch, the principal seceders from strict Hinduism are the Jains, Kanphuttees, Kaprias, and Buddhists. Of all these Hindu sectarians, the great characteristic of their creed is a dread of the destruction of animal life; but whether this great principle arise from their belief in the doctrine of metempsychosis, or whether, with the Persian poet Firdausi, from a pure spirit of benevolent sensibility, they cry,

> "Oh! spare yon emmet, rich in hoarded grain,
> He lives with pleasure, and he dies with pain,"

I am not prepared to judge. Diodorus Siculus relates many curious anecdotes connected with the ordinances and superstitions of the Egyptians, who were by their laws compelled to cherish brute animals; but I am induced to believe, they were more strict in their observance of practical kindness towards them, than are the Hindus; for whatever the tenets of the Hindu religion may be intended to enforce, it is evident, that the system is trivial in its influence on society: the natives of India, although restrained from the actual commission of animal slaughter, are guilty of many and frequent acts of great cruelty towards the brute creation.

The Jains are a peculiar class of ascetics, and well known by the notices of many learned oriental writers. They are frequently to be seen in Cutch, and have temples both at Anjar and Mandavie. Their dress is a simple white garment, descending in full folds from the shoulder to the feet; their heads are bare, and closely shaven; their walk is peculiarly slow, and their eyes are fixed on the ground, in apparently abstract contemplation: they carry in one hand a bunch of feathers, and in the other a small bag, or earthen pot. The most striking peculiarity in their appearance is given by a piece of gauze which they wear over the mouth, to prevent (as they believe) the possibility of any insect entering with the air they breathe. To destroy life, however unintentionally, is considered by the Jains to be an inexpiable sin; and lest they should ignorantly commit such, it is their custom to abstain from food after sunset, to use no water which has not been previously strained, and to sweep the ground

A PRIEST OF THE JAIN SECT.

before their footsteps, lest they should cause death to some minute insect.

The Jains are not polytheists, and pay no respect to the Hindu gods; but although they regard the Brahmins with great hatred, they have many customs in common with them. The Jains burn their dead, pay great reverence to their Gurus, or spiritual teachers, and believe that a life of solitary privation will entitle a devotee to an absorption into the Supreme Being. They profess to believe in one God, whom they endue with the attributes of wisdom, power, eternity, and intuition; but affirm, that the government of the world is independent of him — that matter is eternal — and that the harmony of the visible world is dependent only on natural and organic laws, which must be everlasting.

The finest Jain temples in Western India are built on Mount Aboo, near Deesa, in the province of Marwar. There are others in Kattiwar and Guzzerat, but less beautiful than those on Aboo, which Captain Burnes describes as being built of the purest marble, elaborately and exquisitely carved.

There are also in Cutch three establishments of a monastic order peculiar to the province; and which, although founded at different times, exercise similar charities towards society, and are so far in advance of the generally observed Hindu community, in disinterested and tolerant benevolence, that the social arrangements of the brotherhood become highly worthy of remark. And first in order, are, the Kanphuttees of Denodur.

Denodur is a high and conically shaped hill, overlooking the Runn, from which it has a very picturesque effect; being apparently based on mist, and above displaying a well defined, but very irregular outline. At the foot of this hill dwell the brotherhood of Kanphuttees, in a range of commodious buildings dedicated to the sweet uses of benevolence.

The superior of the Kanphuttees is a peer, placed on the Guardi by the Rao, and presented by him on that occasion with a Khillat, or dress of honour. The brotherhood consist of about twelve Jogies, most of them young men, but old in appearance beyond their years, from the excessive use of opium. The buildings comprise temples, dwelling-houses, and the tombs of the former peers; and are surrounded by a wall turretted and loop-holed for defence — doubtless a necessary precaution in more unsettled times, to guard the peaceful inhabitants against the predatory attacks of the tribes from the opposite side of the Runn, who were wont, like moss-troopers of old, to make forays for the purposes of lawless plunder. In addition to this security, the Denodur establishment is approachable only through a thick jungle, tangled with brushwood and the thorny milk bush.

The principles of these Kanphuttee Jogies is, to feed, shelter, and protect the needy and helpless of all castes, or sects, who may apply for aid, without limit to their time of sojourn, or the magnitude or number of their wants. The expences of their charity are met by the produce of about twenty villages, which are the property of the establishment.

Some of these have been acquired by original grant, and others by purchase; and although, during seasons of great scarcity, the demand on their liberality is proportionate, their revenue fully permits a generous distribution amongst the mendicants, and, like the widow of Sarephath's little cruse of oil, the charitable granaries of Denodur have never failed. In one of their offices are four immense copper cauldrons, in which rice is constantly boiling; and opposite to it is a large room in which the guests seat themselves to partake their favourite food.

The Kanphuttees are vowed to celibacy, and willingly admit any persons as brethren, who submit to the prohibition involved. The fact of giving "hostages to fortune" has, it seems, in all nations, been considered incompatible with the exercise of extraordinary benevolence: domestic cares are supposed to absorb those sentiments of general benevolence which should be dedicated alone to the service of suffering humanity.

There is much in this establishment which strikingly recalls to a European visitor some of the Catholic institutions of continental Europe; for the Kanphuttees of Denodur are in fact hospitallers,

> "And destined to perform from age to age
> The noblest service; welcoming as guests
> All of all nations, and of every faith."

So speaks a modern poet* of the noblest monastic order in the world, that of the Great St. Bernard; but whether the Kanphuttee monks bear any comparison to those of the civilized world, either in the amount of good effected, or in sincere benevolence of purpose, I cannot decide: I speak generally, and have remarked many interesting resemblances between them.

The name of the present peer is Tournath, of the Rubarree† caste. He is about thirty, but bears in his countenance an expression of despondency and premature old age. His dress consists of the usual angrika‡ of white linen, a red Cashmere shawl thrown carelessly over his shoulders, with a turban of rich blue silk: his ornaments are costly, and of the barbaric workmanship of Cutch.

* Rogers. † Shepherd. ‡ Body cloth.

These Jogies take the name of Kanphuttee,* from a peculiar ear-ring they wear, made of rhinoceros horn, agate, or glass, which, from its immense size, painfully distorts the cartilage of the ear. The rich dress I have described is peculiar to the peer: the brotherhood wear the plain brick-dust coloured cloth, common to Fakirs throughout India.†

The isolated position of these really disinterested and amiable beings, is a subject for surprise and conjecture, as the history of their origin remains shrouded in mystery. A legend is recognised throughout Cutch as its sufficient explanation; and although the introduction of mere local fables would be a useless impertinence where other information existed, I cannot think that, in the absence of facts, any subject which tends to illustrate the character, or habits of mind of a peculiar people, will be thought uninteresting, or

* Kanphuttee, or more learnedly *Canp'hata*, from a slit made in the cartilage of the ear, through which a plate of horn, agate, or glass is suspended: Can, or Kan signifying the ear, and p'hata to split.

† The Fakirs of the Gosein sect are distinguished by a wrapper of cloth dyed with red ochre, and by wearing a string of beads called Rudracsha, round the neck. They are worshippers of Siva. The Jogies of the Kanphuttee sect, like the Goseins, are worshippers of Siva, and, therefore, wear a similar garment.

be despised as the insulting imposition of "an old woman's tale."

The following legend affects to be an explanation of the present appearance of the Runn; but I have introduced it in this place, as more immediately connected with the establishment at Denodur. The tradition extends only as far back as 450 years.

LEGEND OF DHURRUMNATH.

During the reign of a mighty Rajah, named Guddeh Sing, a celebrated, and as now supposed deified priest, or hutteet, called Dhurrumnath, came, and in all the characteristic humility of his sect, established a primitive and temporary resting place,* within a few miles of the Rajah's residence at Runn, near Mandăvie. He was accompanied by his adopted son, Ghurreeb Nath.

From this spot, Dhurrumnath despatched his son to seek for charitable contributions from the inhabitants of the town. To this end, Ghurreeb Nath made several visits; but being unsuccessful, and at the same time unwilling that his father should know of the want of liberality in the city, he at each visit purchased food from some limited

* The resting place is called in Cutchee language, the Doonee, and is merely a spot under a tree, or shady bank, where the devotee lights his fire, and arranges his few chattels.

funds of his own. At length, his little hoard failing, on the sixth day he was obliged to confess the deceit he had practised.

Dhurrumnath, on being acquainted with this, became extremely wrath, and vowed, that from that day all the Rajah's Putteen cities should become desolate and ruined.* The tradition goes on to state, that, in due time, these cities were destroyed; when Dhurrumnath, accompanied by his son, left the neighbourhood, and proceeded to Denodur. Finding it a desirable place, he determined on performing Tupseeah, or penance, for twelve years, and chose the form of standing on his head.

On commencing this fanatic determination, he dismissed his son, who established his Doonee in the jungles about twenty miles W. by N. of Bhooj.† After Dhurrumnath had remained Tupseeah for twelve years, he was visited by all the angels from heaven, who besought him to rise: to which he replied, that if he did so, the portion of the country on which his sight would first rest, would become barren; if villages, they

* "Putteen Sub Dutteen," literally, the "wealthy all overthrown." This story of "Putteen Sub Dutteen" is common in all parts of Western India; and Boragud, an ancient city, Raipoor, and others in Cutch, have been said to be so destroyed by means of a Shrap, or curse.

† This spot is said to be now marked.

would disappear ; if woods or fields, they would equally be destroyed. The angels then told him to turn his head to the north-east, where flowed the sea. Upon which he resumed his natural position, and, turning his head in the direction he was told, opened his eyes, when immediately the sea disappeared, the stately ships became wrecks, and their crews destroyed, leaving nothing behind but a barren unbroken desert, known as the Runn. Dhurrumnath, too pure to remain on earth, partook of an immediate and glorious immortality ; being at once absorbed into the spiritual nature of the creating, the finishing, the indivisible, all pervading Brum.

This self-imposed penance of Dhurrumnath has shed a halo of sanctity around the hill of Denodur, and was doubtless the occasion of its having been selected as a fitting site for a Jogie establishment ; the members of which, it is probable, were originally the attendants on a small temple that had been erected, and which still remains, on the highest point of the hill, on the spot where the holy Dhurrumnath is said to have performed his painful Tupseeah.

THE KAPRIAS OF MHURR.

In connection with the Denodur establishment, as productive of similar acts of benevolence, is the sect of Kaprias at Mhurr, which is a small village near the Runn, in a north-westernly direction from Bhooj. Their government, and the object of their religious veneration, are peculiar, and consequently deserving of notice. The sect is supposed to be about eighteen hundred years old; but its origin is involved in obscurity. In number the fraternity amount to about one hundred and twenty, and they are governed by a Rajah, who enjoys many immunities and privileges: amongst others, that of retaining his seat, even when visited by the Rao of Cutch.* They have also a singular custom connected with their Rajah, which is, that should he leave the

* The Rao visits the establishment of Kaprias once in every year, in accordance with a vow made by his mother, at the shrine of Ashapura, whilst he was suffering from an attack of small pox. Vows of this nature are very common in Cutch; and it was during his mother's subsequent illness, that the Rao vowed to build a temple at Rhoda, near Bhooj, if the Ranee were spared. It happened that her disease left her, and a beautiful temple to Parvati proved the piety and filial affection of his Highness. These vows are made during the illness of a beloved object; but after death, the greatest proof a rich native can give of his grief, is to feed, and make presents to the Brahmins. Immediately after the decease of the Rao's mother, thousands of Brahmins came into Bhooj from every part of Cutch; and between their feasting for the ten appointed days of mourning, and donations made to the temple at D'waka, it is supposed that the Rao expended more than a lac of coories.

village during the day, he cannot return to it until after sunset. Like the Kanphuttees, the Kaprias are sworn to celibacy; but the Rajah may adopt sons, who succeed him on the Guardi. Any Hindu desiring to join the fraternity is at liberty to do so; and the form of his inauguration is simple: he takes the vows, drinks Kusumba,* and joins in the feast given on the occasion. They possess five villages, the revenues of which they devote, like the monks of Denodur, to the charitable purpose of feeding all who apply for assistance. They present opium to visitors of rank, and are provident for the wants of brute animals as well as those of men. The Kaprias bury all their dead; but the Rajah, whose obsequies they honour with a funeral pyre, they mourn the loss of for twelve days. At the expiration of that time, they receive his successor, with feasting and merriment. It is stated, that this sect enjoyed the peculiar protection of Gund hurvu Senu,† the son of Indra; but I believe this is not a very generally received tradition.

In the midst of their village is a temple dedicated to Parvati,‡ known in Cutch as the goddess Ashapura. It contains a monstrous image, which forms the particular object of their adoration. It

* Liquefied opium.

† See legend of "Vere and Vicram."

‡ The wife of Vishnu.

is an immense block of black stone, six feet high, and the same in width, of a most uncouth form: the base of it has two large excrescences, and the upper part somewhat resembles an awkward looking leg of mutton. There is no rational account to be obtained of the origin of this image: it is said to have suddenly started from the ground, on a spot where the goddess had slain a giant in single combat; but it bears neither carving nor inscription. It is smeared all over with the ubiquitous pigment of red ochre, with which, or with chalk, the Hindus hide and deface their most beautiful, as well as most monstrous, remains of antiquity. The people state that this huge stone idol has occupied its present place since the Treta Yuga;* and as this age, according to Hindu computation, was somewhat more than 432,000 years before the Deluge, it might be rather difficult to collate sufficient evidence to afford any very authentic information respecting its origin!

* The Hindus divide their ages into vast cycles: that of the Maha Yuga, or great age, is divided into four Yugas, or ages, of less extent; the idea of which seems to have originated similarly with that of the golden, silver, brazen, and iron ages of the Greeks, "according to the different proportions of virtue prevailing on earth." In the Satya Yuga, or age of virtue, four parts, or all mankind, were supposed to be good; in the Treta Yuga, three. — For a very learned dissertation on this subject, see HALES's "*Analysis of Chronology.*"

The Kaprias themselves are a fat, smiling, good-natured, set of people, indolent and merry ; but, unlike "the jovial friars of orders grey," their food is of the simplest kind, taken in sparing quantities.

ARAB SOLDIERS,

In the pay of the Rao of Cutch.

CHAPTER XI.

THE MILITARY TRIBES OF CUTCH.

Feodal Tenure.—Jharrejahs, and their Retainers, the Grasias.—Rajpoot Women. — Origin of the Jharrejahs. — Supposed Murder of the Princess Kesser Bhye. — Meyannahs, or Warriors. — Soodahs. — Beauty of the Soodah Women. — Intermarriages. — Jharrejah Costume. — Arms. — Eastern Practice of Dyeing Beards and Moustaches.

I HAVE already remarked on the similarity of the government of Cutch to that of the feodal times in England,* and have explained that the Rao is in fact the lord paramount of a set of chiefs called Jharrejahs, who are of the Rajpoot tribe, and sworn to hold their lands as feodal tenures, giving military service to the Rao, whenever the emergencies of the state require it.

The immediate retainers of these Cutchee barons owe similar allegiance to their several heads; and, acknowledging them as supreme, would feel bound to support their power, even in opposition to the Rao, in case of rebellion or civil war. These retainers are called Grasias, and

* See note on the custom of "Mohsulsee," Chap. II.

are invested with the government of inferior villages.

The Jharrejahs are a singularly fine race of men, naturally robust, and peculiarly warlike in dress and bearing; but in their habits dissipated, proud, and cruel. Some years have now passed, since Cutch has been a scene of contention for federal rights ; and during this interval, the Jharrejahs have sunk into a state of apathy and sensual indulgence. Addicted to the use of opium and spirituous liquors, those amongst them who are much advanced in life betray, in their haggard countenances, the common effects of these habits of intemperance and excess.

The Rajpoot women, who marry these men for the sake of their estates, are handsome, high-spirited, and very superior to the other castes of native women. I speak, however, only from representation; as the Jharrejahs seclude their women, and I have not had any opportunity of being introduced to these Calypsos of the land. But it is said, that "the sacred harem's silent tower" is too often the scene of desperate intrigue ; and that "fair as the first who fell of woman-kind," the dark-eyed Rajpootni frequently becomes the victim of her wayward and evil passions. Beautiful and high-born, these women feel little sympathy or affection for their debauched lords, and are accused of diverting the tedium of their lives by intrigues and associations of a most degrading nature.

The Rajpoot Jharrejahs derive their name from Jharrah, a Mahomedan of rank, who, coming to Cutch, which was at that time inhabited by pastoral tribes, became enslaved by the loveliness of a fair Hindu, whom he married. After his death, his young widow was expelled from his family at the instance of his Mahomedan wives; and, like another Hagar, she departed, with her infant son, to seek refuge from the more merciful. Her son grew; he took unto himself wives of the daughters of the land; and his descendants established themselves in independence, taking the title of Jharrejahs. In time, the chief of this tribe assumed the title of Jam,* and held it for many years, until expelled from Cutch into Kattiwar, by the fiat of the celebrated Emperor Akbar. It is, therefore, difficult to decide, whether the Jharrejahs should be classed as Hindus or Moslems; more particularly as the Rao, who is the head of the Bhyaud,† pays reverence to both modes of worship;‡ and the "Order of the Fish"|| was be-

* A Mahomedan distinction common in Sindh.

† Brotherhood.

‡ The Rao himself says that out of about two thousand Jharrejahs, he does not think three of them know what their religion is.

|| Called the "Mahi Muratib," and borne above the royal standard.

stowed on the early princes of Cutch by the Emperor of Delhi, on their pledging themselves to defray the expenses of all pilgrims travelling to Mecca. The Hindus also form family connexions with the Moslems. A sister of Rao Bharmuljee's, a princess distinguished by her wisdom and masculine understanding, married a Jam of the Noanugger family, in Kattiwar, but died shortly after her marriage; and it was suspected that she had been destroyed, by poison introduced into her slippers. The jealous passions of the harem's inmates could ill brook the sway of this highly gifted and most unfortunate woman. With a spirit uncontaminated by the presence of evil, Kesser Bhye had passed her life in a court degraded by crime, and all her energies and affections had been exerted, to save the victims of her brother's dark and guilty passions. Often had his blood-stained hand been stayed from the commission of deeper crime, by the entreaties of his gentle sister; and though herself the victim of dark and private treachery, the name of Kesser Bhye is still hallowed throughout the province. It would appear, then, that the Cutch Jharrejah shares the proportions of his divided faith, according to the origin of his ancestry. He believes in the Koran, worships saints, swears by Allah, and lives in Mahomedan style: the worship of Vishnu is, however, skilfully mingled with all this, and the whole forms a curious *mélange* of religious faith..

Another caste of warriors, called Meyannahs, were originally shepherds, but, exchanging the crook for the spear, have become a fierce and warlike people, celebrated as plunderers, and as being ready to take any military service, if well paid, and suffered to pillage without restraint. The hand of the Meyannah mercenary is equally ready for the warrior's spear, or the assassin's dagger; and he never fails his employer, or hesitates to perform the most atrocious deed, if proportionately recompensed. In the reign of the Rao Bharmuljee, during a civil war, when the British power was required to quell the contentions of the feodal chiefs, the Meyannahs came to Anjar, and poisoned the wells, by which many men and cattle died. These men are Mahomedans, and may be mustered to the amount of three thousand warriors.

The Soodahs, although not a provincial tribe, may be mentioned here, as being intimately connected with Cutch, both by their predatory excursions and the intermarriages of their beautiful daughters with the Rajpoot Jharrejahs. This tribe reside in Wandhs, or grass huts, on the great desert of the Thurr,* in a state of peculiar

* The Thurr bounds Cutch to the north, and divides it from Sindh.

wretchedness and privation. Ignorant and barbarous, they pass their lives as shepherds, frequently assembling in hordes, and making forays across the northern Runn, into the neighbouring provinces, and driving back the cattle of the villagers to their Wandhs, where they for a time subsist in peace, on milk, and the few vegetables of the jungle

The Soodahs find their principal source of riches in the beauty of their daughters, for one of whom rich Mahomedans will frequently pay ten thousand rupees. Rajahs and wealthy chieftains despatch their emissaries, as Abraham sent his servant, to seek a wife for Isaac of the daughters of Nahor; and, like Bethuel, the Soodah father offers no objection to a wealthy suitor, but, on the contrary, robs his son-in-law, before his camels and servants depart. Beside the wells, and in the hovels of the Thurr, full many a flower of female loveliness would blush unseen, but for the fame of their surpassing beauty, which claims and maintains its ascendancy, and transplants the blossom of the desert to bloom amidst the gorgeous pomp of a royal harem. It is said, that the Soodah women are artful and cunning; and that by these qualities they gain a powerful influence over the minds of their liege lords, to whom they bear little affection. The Soodah wife of a Rajpoot cares only for her son; and report avers, hesitates little to dispose of the father, to invest his heir with the estate.

The Soodahs themselves never intermarry, but form alliances with the people of the neighbouring provinces. From this circumstance, it is reasonable to infer that the daughters inherit their fairness from their paternal ancestry; as otherwise, it would be less uncommon. In Cutch the crime of infanticide prevents our judging of what charms may descend to the female offspring of the Soodah women; but I should imagine they would be many, as the Rajpoot Jharrejahs are naturally a very handsome race, although enervated by intemperate habits. Too proud to be virtuous, these haughty chiefs are cruel and debauched in times of peace, and terrible in the days of strife. No deed of blood, no act of treachery, is then too dark for their evil passions to plan and execute. Pity is unknown in the schemes of their vengeance; and the history of Cutch has tales so full of horror in its annals, as at once prove, that where the Jharrejah's

> "frown of hatred darkly fell,
> Hope withering fled—and mercy sighed farewell."

These people are remarkable for large turbans and long moustaches, which they constantly draw out, and smooth between the fingers and thumb. I am speaking within bounds, in saying, I have seen a Rajpoot Jharrejah's moustache half a yard in length. They are very proud of this acquisition, and carefully comb and dress their moustaches into two separate locks, which descend to their breast.* Their arms are a spear, shield, and short sword; they ride admirably; and in olden times, thirty thousand cavalry have been collected in three days, to protect their feodal rights.†

> "Thus join the bands, whom mutual wrong,
> And fate, and fury drive along."

* The Rajpoots, who consider it a disgrace to wear either white beards or grey moustaches, when they become so in old age, dye them with a preparation of indigo. Thus dyed, however, after a few days, the beard, or moustache, assumes a purple tint, and finally fades to a pale plum colour, far from being either deceptive or ornamental. The process of dyeing is, I believe, tedious; and the artist compels his patient to sit many hours under the indigo treatment, with his head wrapt up in wet plantain leaves. Indigo does not grow in Cutch, but is procured at a very cheap rate from Sindh, where it flourishes luxuriantly.

† This gathering of the Jharrejahs and Grasias in so short a time, is effected by means of express-camels, which travel swiftly, and find every man ready. The name of the express camel is, Chupper.

CHAPTER XII.

CASTLES IN CUTCH.

Picturesque Sites.—Feodal Times and Tenures.—Reflections on the Feodal System.—Treachery of a Mahratta Chief.

"His look
Haughty as his pile, high built and proud."
Samson Agonistes.

THE majority of towns in Cutch are overlooked by castles, which were in olden times the strong holds of the feodal chiefs, but of late years have been deserted. They are well built, and usually in very picturesque positions; sometimes on the banks of a sedgy river, or on the wooded borders of a tank. Their site is generally on a gently sloping eminence, their turreted battlements overlooking a bright and fertile plain, in which the husbandmen are labouring in their fields, and the oxen bearing their full charged mussochs* from the shaded wells. Such are these strong places in the time of peace: a picturesque addition to a

* Leathern bags for containing water.

pastoral scene, a bold back-ground to a landscape full of repose and beauty; but, let the mind of the observer revert to other days—let it recall these fortresses, as they would have appeared to him in times of aristocratic and desolating tyranny, when each petty chief denied his allegiance to his sovereign, and here sheltered himself with his immediate retainers, protecting the robber and the outlaw, and saving the murderer from the price of blood; let it recall the time, when the fierce and rebellious lords of these strong forts swept from beneath their portals, through these valleys now so peaceful, and by the power of most unjust oppression, wrested the labour of his hand from the cultivator, massacred his flocks, and carried fire and desolation into his dwelling; then indeed, will the scene appear to darken, and contemplation bring with it sweeping remembrances of evil, which overshadow the present, and load it with dismay.

In all countries where the feodal tenure has led to the assertion of individual rights and baronial rebellion, similar fortresses are common; and, at this remote period, they are rich in poetic and historic interest. Even in civilized countries, where these monuments of a barbarous age abound, many of them, being of undoubted antiquity, are indebted more to tradition than to historical record.

There is a sort of spirit-stirring interest, which always attaches itself to these wild and reckless times, and from it has undoubtedly arisen poetic beauty of no mean kind. Many of the warlike deeds of a barbarous people are preserved only in their bardic fragments, and known to us by tradition; and, like the chiefs of the north, the Jharrejahs of Cutch are said to have delighted to hear the deeds of their ancestors sung and rehearsed in ancient story. A collection of these "tales of the times of old" would be highly interesting: they are still, I believe, recited by the native bards; but the feodal spirit sleeps, and its warlike deeds have passed away like a dream. The time which allowed the wicked to wax mighty and to oppress their fellows has departed, and with it the historical records of the feodal barons, of the ready serf, and of the castellated fortress; the dungeon gloom and the treacherous portcullis have faded in the distance; and, in our halcyon days of peace and civilization, seem to deserve rather the character of romantic legends, than of realities even of the darkest age.

It has been considered, that the manners of the feodal times were advantageous to the human character: true, they may have been so, when giving birth to the feelings of honour, truth, and loyalty, howsoever rude in their development; but the selfishness of an Asiatic cannot allow him to view the system as a social contract for the mutual and better protection of the integral parts of a state: he regards it only as a source of individual power, and as a means by which he may nourish his independence, and foster his rebellious spirit, in times of anarchy and confusion. Numerous are the records of the faithless conduct of chieftains, in times when each becomes jealous of the rest, and considers no form of treachery too base, which may enable him to gain power over their lives and property.

A case is well known, where one of these savage warriors, having deluded a neighbouring chief into his fortress, under the mask of desiring an amicable conference, folded his guest in his mailed arms, according to the mode of Eastern salutation, and then, dead to every principle of honour, rent his foe asunder, before the eyes of his retainers, while the flag of truce was floating from the battlements.*

This, and many others, are instances of private treachery; and native violations of public faith are well known to the British government, as always tending to preclude any reliance on their promised aid. The confederacies of the Mahratta empire are, perhaps, the most generally known,

* This is related of Sevajee, the Mahratta chief: the crime was perpetrated in the magnificent fortress of Purtabghur, situated between Bombay and the Mahabuleshwar hills.

and present some of the darkest pages in the annals of our Indian conquests. Instead of supporting the power of their lord against foreign oppression, these chiefs commonly broke into open rebellion, acknowledging no allegiance but to their own ambition, nor any loyalty, but to that selfish policy which promised its advancement.

On a smaller field for action, but precisely on the same principles, have the Jharrejah chiefs of Cutch held their several fiefs, devastating the province with civil war, calling to their aid the mercenary warriors of the desert, and suffering them to carry carnage and desolation over their country; making poison and the dagger the ready instruments for the gratification of their savage vengeance.

These times are passed away. Cutch is protected by a subsidiary force of Company's troops; the local chiefs have entered into treaties with the British government, which have left them only nominal power; the estates are cultivated, the strongholds deserted, and peace flourishes throughout the land.

CHAPTER XIII.

INFANTICIDE IN CUTCH.

Pride, the Origin of the Cold-blooded and Unnatural Crime of Infanticide.—Indifference of Rajpoot Mothers to their Offspring.—British Treaty for the Preservation of Female Infants.—Disproportion of Male and Female Population.—Professed Intentions of the Rao.—Insufficiency of Coercive Measures.—Barriers of Caste.

PRIDE works with fiendish violence in the minds of the Rajpoot Jharrejahs, and has goaded them to the unceasing exercise of an immemorial custom, vile and unnatural. Indeed, it is hardly possible to imagine, how any passion of man could be sufficient to impel him to the perpetual and cold-blooded perpetration of a crime so opposed to the instincts of our nature. Affection and tenderness to offspring are not a sentiment which civilization has implanted in man. Parental care is the indissoluble tie which secures the objects of creation; it is the voice of mercy, which cries aloud in the heart of every created being, and makes it yearn towards the helpless, and protect the weak ; it is the great law of love, inspiring every thing which has life; and the more savage the nature of the parent, so is it mercifully ordained, that this beautiful and necessary passion should be proportionably developed. All nature obeys its dictates, but this monster man, who, deaf to its suggestions, sacrifices his child, his helpless little one, at the shrine of that Moloch of his heart, the pride of caste.

The Jharrejahs are unable to give any account of this cruel and inhuman custom. They state it to have been a general usage since a marriage of one of their chief's daughters was followed by disgrace and ruin to some of the Jharrejah families.

They consider, in fact, that it is a loss of character, when a Jharrejah's daughter marries any man,* none being considered her equal ; and as, in India, celibacy, in the opinion of the natives, is synonymous with crime, no alternative remains, but to quench the young life of their female offspring.

> "That monster custom, who all sense doth eat
> Of habit's devil,"

* A Rajpoot can take a daughter to wife only of the tribe below him, and give a daughter to the tribe above him : to intermarry in a tribe is considered incest ; and as the Jharrejahs have no tribe above them, infanticide becomes their only resource.

makes all things easy; and the young Rajpoot mother, holding her first-born to her breast, suffers its natural sustenance to be poisoned at its source, and sees her little infant sink into the sleep of death, within her arms.* Strange, that nature's strongest instincts can be so lulled! strange, that a Soodah woman should thus calmly extinguish a life, which she has been taught by her own people to prize so highly! and that no sob of agony should convulse her heart, as her innocent and helpless babe closes its little life in her first embrace. Alas! far from this, it is remarked that a Rajpoot wife becomes even more tenacious of this custom than her husband, and makes no effort to preserve the life of her hapless infant.

Despicable as these wretches are, from the constant exercise of every vice, they imagine themselves superior to all other castes; and although their sensual passions lead them to seek wives from a tribe of plunderers, they consider that no caste is worthy to receive their daughters, or to be honoured with their alliance. Not only the Jharrejahs, but all Mahomedans in Cutch, who pride themselves on being descended from the same original head, commit, daily, these deliberate murders. Great and various have been the efforts made by the British Government to prevent

* The general method in use by the Rajpoot nurses is to apply opium to the breast of the mother.

this dreadful practice; and the Jharrejahs have entered into a treaty with us, agreeing to forbid the destruction of their female infants, on condition that we respect the prejudices of the Hindus, and their religious reverence for the ox and cow. This agreement has been held sacred on our part, and the slaughter of these animals is forbidden throughout the province; but it is feared, that our forbearance has done little to suppress the amount of crime. It is wholly impossible to institute strict inquiries into the domestic affairs of a Jharrejah's family; their women are secluded, and the harem's privacy is inviolable. According to the terms of the treaty, the Jharrejahs are bound to return a yearly census of their tribe; but we have no means of ascertaining its truth, and the male population so far exceeds the female,* that no doubt can exist, but that these murders are still common. It has been calculated, that there was annually in this province a destruction of one thousand lives, and that amongst eight thousand Jharrejahs, the number of their women did not exceed thirty. This very small number were preserved, some by accident, and some by the Jharrejah believers in Vishnu. There is little hope of the abolition of this fearful custom, until reproved by the power of ex-

* This is peculiarly striking in passing through their villages.

ample. Were this crime to be discontinued by any of their tribe, possessing influence and high caste, the haughty Jharrejah might allow his prejudice to be removed, and feel the spirit of an unknown tenderness awakened in his heart; but no treaties will avail to secure his faith, and no threats will prevent his perpetual evasion of them. The Rao of Cutch, who is the Lord Paramount of the Bhyaud of Jharrejahs, has declared, that should a daughter be born to his house, he will preserve and nurture it, as an evidence of his desire to correct so demoralizing and rank an offence. The Rao is an amiable man, tender and affectionate in all the relations of life; his enlightened views, and his gentleness of nature, have combined to render this custom distasteful to him; and, being unenforced by any religious injunctions, I have no doubt his Highness is sincere, and I trust, that his example may afford the required precedent, to emancipate the Jharrejahs' daughters from their cruel doom. In common, however, with all improvement in this degraded country, the effect produced will be of very gradual and tardy development; and mere political influence will never compass it. Means will be found to evade enquiry and evidence; or, supposing the existing evil to be suppressed, others, calculated to produce the same effects, will succeed it. Well adapted measures, founded on the experiences of those which have proved hitherto inefficient, may prevent the systematic sacrifice of infant life; but will neither induce the Rajpoot to renounce his prejudices, nor to sacrifice his pride of caste, by suffering his daughters to become the wives of those whom he considers so immeasurably beneath him. Rather than see his blooming daughter unite herself to her inferior, or bring disgrace on her family by a life of celibacy, the Rajpoot father will take other means to preserve his caste from this dreaded degradation. The daughters of the people of Canaan were sacrificed, at adult age, before the altars of Baal; and will not the recesses of the harem conceal the blood that may flow, to wash away the stain which has fallen on the pride of caste? The extinction of life is held as a venial crime in Mahomedan privacy. The poisoned slipper, or the sherbet bowl, becomes the "cup of immortality"* to the doomed one. Enquiry is never made, and remorse is unfelt. Oh! matched with these,

> "The rudest brute that roams Siberia's wild
> Has feelings pure, and polished as a gem;
> The bear is civilized — the wolf is mild—
> And whom for this at last must we condemn?"

* Called the "Amreeta Cup"—Amreeta is the sacred name of amber, in its perfect state; it was obtained on the churning of the ocean by the Hindu gods, whom it rendered immortal, and to whom it solely belongs.

Oh! say not nature—she is gentle in her dictates, and true to her objects; she is the same in all climes; and however social laws may vary, benevolence, conscientiousness, and veneration, are her principles. Caste is the agent of misery, and here to be condemned as the only, but the mountainous obstacle, which prevents the light of nature from streaming on the understandings of these degraded beings. The barrier of caste, then, must be removed; years, ay ages must elapse ere its corner-stone be loosened; and the herculean labour can be attempted only by the power of that knowledge which has broken away mountains of error, and is still every where employed, in carrying down the stream of time its remaining rubbish. The Jharrejah's savage nature must be tamed by some better occupation than is afforded by the brutalizing indulgence of his opium and his hookah; he must learn, as many not less savage have done, to feel the responsibilities of his state, to understand the relative rights of man, the harmonies of nature, the necessities and duties of the social compact; and above all, to appreciate the value of this knowledge, and to learn to regard his brother man with respect, as he sees him the possessor of this mental wealth, and no longer to value him only for his superiority of caste, his muscular strength, or the number of his followers.

I am aware that these opinions with reference to so barbarous a people may appear Utopian; but thus have all great schemes, as shadowed forth ages before their time of trial came, been deemed. Of late years civilization has advanced with rapid power, and reflection has been busy on the means of giving to it even a greater impetus. Our hopes, therefore, have a just foundation, that systems will be tried, ere they are condemned; and that henceforth, none will be considered Utopian, but such as may have failed.

CHAPTER XIV.

RUINS IN CUTCH.

Ruins of the Cities of Poorugud, Goontre, and Wagum Chowrah.—Palace of Poorugud.—Style of Architecture.—Temple of Mahadeo.—Legend of the Rookhees, or Seven Holy Men of Damascus.—Effects of Hindu Superstition.

"The labour of an age in piled stones."

THE principal ruins in Cutch are those of three cities in a westernly direction from Bhooj; and they are known as Poorugud, Goontre, and Wagum Chowrah. Poorugud has the remains of buildings which prove it to have once been entitled to notice as a place of wealth and importance. The site of the walls of the city is easily distinguishable; but time has destroyed all vestige of human habitation, except the palace, mint, and a small temple sacred to Mahadeo, without the gates. The style of the architecture of these agreeing with that of some other buildings in

Cutch, whose origin has been traced, this city is supposed to be about nine hundred years old.

The Palace, which, like many of the Hindu buildings, was erected before the knowledge of the power of the arch was known to their architects, consists of a double tier of apartments, and a flat terraced roof, built wholly of solid blocks of a very hard brown stone; many of which are of the unusual size of ten feet in length, and from two to three feet wide. The upper story is supported by eighty-four pillars, composed of single blocks of stone, adorned with square capitals richly carved. The roof is singularly heavy, and has in various places fallen in. The stones bear no appearance of having ever been cemented; and it is also curious, that no wood has been used in any part of the structure. The upper and lower apartments are not connected by any staircase, but were gained by ladders; the lower ceiling being open in the centre, the apartments above forming a sort of gallery round it. The whole structure is low, not exceeding the height of twenty feet, and is clumsy and ponderous in its general effect, although great taste and much architectural beauty have been displayed in its various ornaments.

The Mint is a heap of rubbish; and the entire site of the dwelling-houses has become like a neglected garden, tangled with weeds and bushes, flourishing in rank luxuriance, throwing up their branches from between the masses of stone which have checked and turned aside the growth of their tough and enduring roots. The many-tinted lichen, "wi' its mantle o' green," has shed the beauty of freshness and grace over mouldering walls, and heaps of rubbish,

> "Which the snake and the lizard inhabit alone,
> With the twilight bat, from the old hollow stone."

In days of yore, architectural skill would seem to have been a dangerous talent to its possessor; as it is stated, that King Poom, for whom the city was built, was so delighted with its beauty, that he ordered the hands of the architect to be cut off, lest other princes should possess cities equal to his own.

The temple dedicated to Mahadeo is in the form of a pagoda, and contains several exquisitely beautiful carvings of figures, supposed to represent Krishna, accompanied by his favourite wife Rookminee. These figures are placed in compartments resembling gothic niches, and are thrown out, in full relief, from the original stone on which they are sculptured.

A tradition is extant, by which the ruined state of the city is, in the opinion of the natives, satisfactorily accounted for. They state, that during the reign of Poom, the founder of the city known as Poorugud, or more properly, *Poom-ka-Gud*,* a sect, composed of seven holy men called Rookhees, came from Damascus to Cutch, that they might be enabled to worship, in solitary contemplation, the attributes of their god Juck, who, gratified by their zealous homage, bestowed on them supernatural power.

It would seem, that the power of these holy recluses had bestowed the much-desired boon of a son, on the wife of the chief musician at the court of King Poom; and the queen, who was herself pining for want of an heir to the throne of her husband, learnt the particulars of the affair from the wife of the musician, and, in the hope of equal good fortune, herself determined to apply to the Rookhees. Fearing, however, that her wishes might meet with opposition from the king, she directed a private passage to be excavated between the palace and the sacred hill of the Rookhees.† After proffering her services to the holy men, she made her request, that they would bestow on her a son; but it was met by the assurance, that the gods would be deaf to her prayers, until the oppression of the king her husband over his people should be expiated by sacrifices, and by a perusal of the Holy Shastrus.

* "Gud," literally meaning, fort; "Poom-ka-Gud," the fort of Poom.

† The entrance to this is still shown.

The queen immediately prepared a sacrifice, to which she invited the seven Rookhees; but, coming in haste, they forgot the deer skins on which they slept, and which contained the essence of their supernatural power. Thus they fell into the hands of Poom, who surprised them before the conclusion of the sacrifice.

The king ordered them to be fastened together, and compelled them to trample on iron hooks, as bullocks are made to tread out the grain. One Rookhee, getting released, ran to the top of a hill, and called his god Juck to his assistance. Juck, with his seventy-one brothers, and a sister called Sarurec, came from Damascus, and seated himself on the hill where the Rookhees had worshipped. The hill, however, unable to sustain so much purity, began to sink, and he left it, calling it Nunnow; and so moved on from hill to hill from the same necessity, and bestowed on each the name it now bears. At last, finding the search for a resting place vain, they each took a stone from their horse's grain bag, and, seating themselves on it, remonstrated with Poom, from a hill called Kuckerbit, where a temple has been built in honour of Juck.

Finding Poom refuse to let the Rookhees go, Juck ordered his brothers to shoot him; but an amulet which he wore rendered their arrows harmless. Observing this, the sister of Juck transformed herself into a mosquito, and bit Poom, so that he called for water to bathe. Juck seized the opportunity, and as he laid aside his amulet, caused an arrow to be fired on the corner of the building where Poom bathed, so that it fell, and crushed him. On the death of the king, Juck cursed the city — its people, and its stones. Thus the city of Poom-ka-gud was built, and deserted in two years; and the people of the present time dare not remove its stones, lest the curse of Juck fall also upon them.

Here ends the tradition. It is worthy of remark, that about the time when Poomkagud is supposed to have been built, many earthquakes were felt in various parts of India; it is, therefore, very probable that the city owes its destruction to one of these phenomena. It is to be regretted, that the superstitions of the people prevent any attempt being made to excavate the mint or palace, where, it is probable, coins and other articles of curiosity might be found, highly interesting to Asiatic researchers.

Traditions of this nature, however, produce one good effect, which the lover of picturesque and hoar antiquity will truly appreciate: it preserves the beautiful evidence of now forgotten arts from wanton destruction at the hand of the ignorant and tasteless; and leaves the interesting relics of the past, unmarred by renovation, to gain new interest by the gradual inroads of time, which will not fail to wreath the crumbling works of man with a rich tracery of nature's foliage, leaving it still,

> "A noble wreck, in ruinous perfection."

The ruins of Goontre and Wagum Chowrah are of small extent, and demand not any particular notice.

CHAPTER XV.

PILGRIMS.

Pilgrimage to Mecca.—Privation and Fatigue.—Usbeck Tartars.—Mahomedans of Yarcund.—Mahomed Niyaz.—The Kebla Nimah.—Pilgrim Presents.—Hindu Pilgrims.—Penance of Five Brahmins.—Peeran Peer, the Saint of Bagdat. — Tombs.—Mendicant Fakirs.—Cause of Hindu Indifference to Life. — Tenets of the Hindu Faith. — Horrible Penances. — Hindu Fanatic. — Remarkable Custom of Traga.

"I would forthwith, and, in a Pilgrim's weeds,
Visit that holy shrine."

CUTCH is a considerable thoroughfare for such religiously disposed moslems as, from the countries of Sindh, Kandahar, Cabool, &c., desire to offer up their vows at the holy shrine of Mecca, and be refreshed with the pure waters of the Zemzem. Mandavie, from its constant intercourse by means of trade with the ports of the Red Sea, offers them peculiar advantages by this route; and, as I have already mentioned, the Rao of Cutch is pledged, by the terms of an old treaty, to afford all Mahomedan pilgrims free convoy. Many of these poor fanatics perish on the way, from fatigue, climate, and privation, combined with the effects of pestilential disease, which constantly attacks their caravans. They experience, however, the greatest consolation in the idea of meeting death as true Mahomedans should, with their faces towards Mecca.

They, whose idea of a pilgrim is united with that of a sedate philosophical being, who wends his solitary way, scanning society in its various moods, yet heedless of its lines — demanding, by virtue of his saintly errand, shelter from the noble, and respect from his retainers — would with difficulty recognise the pilgrim character as it is displayed in the poor, slothful, unimaginative beings, who form so large a fraternity amongst the worshippers of the Prophet; and it is grievous to observe so many young men, able to fulfil the active duties of life, desert their families and country, and traverse deserts, and endure so much, in the discharge of a revered object, subsisting by the way on the charity of the more industrious. The class of these wanderers, as seen in Cutch, is usually of a common order; or, if they possess wealth, it is left at home. Their general dress is a dark-coloured cotton zaboot,* which, with a

* A zaboot is a large loose cloak, with wide and hanging sleeves.

hookah, staff, and compass, completes their travelling equipment.

The most interesting pilgrims I have seen in Cutch were a party of Usbeck Tartars from Yarcund, one of the western frontier possessions of China. The second volume of Captain Burnes's very intelligent and interesting work on Bokhara gives us a curious history of the domestic arrangements of the Yarcundees, which perfectly coincides with the description personally afforded me by these pilgrims.

"The Mahomedans of Yarcund," says this amusing writer, "appear to differ from their brethren elsewhere; for the fair sex have a power and influence not known in other places. They take the seat of honour in a room, associate freely with the men, and do not veil; they wear high-heeled boots richly ornamented; their head-dress is described as being handsome, being a high tiara of cloth: the features of the fair ones themselves are said to be most beautiful. When a Bokhara merchant visits Yarcund, he marries one of these beauties during his sojourn in the city; and the pair separate as they joined, quite as a matter of convenience, when he leaves the city. There, wives are as cheap as beautiful, and purchased at a premium of two or three tillas, (twelve or eighteen rupees); and the merchants, long after leaving the country, sing the praises of the fair ones of Yarcund."

These arrangements are, indeed, singularly liberal, and very unlike the restraints usually imposed by Mahomedan jealousy. I have not yet learnt by what mighty magic these fair dames succeeded in securing so great an emancipation.

The most intelligent and pleasing of the pilgrim party was Mahomed Niyaz, a native of Yarcund, and who, I was assured, had the genuine physiognomy of an Usbeck of Toorkistan. The expression of his countenance was animated and benevolent; his complexion rather fairer than is common amongst the natives of India, and marked with that flatness of general contour which is characteristic of the Tartar physiognomy. This was his first pilgrimage; but one of his companions had made the Haj, as it is called, before, and in consequence was compelled to forego the use of the two Asiatic luxuries, coffee and the hookah. They were all dressed in large zaboots of white cotton, with small turbans neatly folded and of the same material; but they assured me, their usual dress was of rich stuffs, and of very superior fashion. They seemed particularly gratified by being made subjects of attention, and gave some very animated descriptions of their country. In proceeding to Mecca, their steps are directed to the Kebla of their hopes, by means of a small compass, which they call the Kebla Nimah, or, "director to the House of God."* This little instrument is enclosed in a silver case, about the size of a sparrow's egg: the dial of the compass is not divided, or marked, like our own; but the hand is in the form of a flying dove, whose beak, true to its duty, points always towards Mecca. This, the travellers ascribe to the influence of the Prophet, and follow its guidance over desert plains with as much implicit confidence, as the mariner, secure in the power of science, tracks his way over pathless and unknown seas.

On taking leave of us, the poor Yarcundees entreated our acceptance of some trifling presents,

* The object of the Mahomedan Pilgrim's visit to Mecca is to kiss the "Hujr-ul-Uswud," or black stone, contained in what they call, the House of God. It is incumbent on a Mahomedan to visit Mecca, as soon as he can provide for his family, and afford the expenses of the journey. It is also necessary that a Pilgrim should obtain the consent of his family; for, if he approach the "Hujr-ul-Uswud" without

in conformity with the customs of their country. These consisted of a Chinese writing box,* a rice-paper fan, and a chowrie† made from the tail of the celebrated "Yak," of Tartary. The hair of the chowrie was long, and of a silvery hue: it was let into a black handle roughly carved in the Chinese style.

Hindu pilgrims are very numerous: they come from the distant parts of India, to perform penances at D'waka,‡ and at other places which bear a holy character. A common custom amongst them is that of taking a vow of measuring their length to a place of supreme sanctity, far removed from the spot where the vow is made; and in this tedious and painful way, they are said to travel over vast tracks of country. I am disposed to believe that their system of surveying is very correct only in the neighbourhood of inhabited districts. However, it is daily proved, that fanaticism renders its devotee capable of great suffer-

this, he is guilty of a great sin. Some of the Pilgrims visit Mecca seven times, during their life. Many are sincere in their devotion; but others go, merely to barter relics on their return, and numbers fall into the hands of the Arabs, who plunder and ill-treat them, in the most cruel manner. A full description of the objects of reverence at Mecca may be seen in the Preliminary Discourse to MR. SALE'S *Koran*.

* A kullumdaun.

† A sort of whisk, used to disperse flies.

‡ A very holy temple on the coast of Kattiwar.

ing and privation ; and though India is over-run by a tribe of miserable Fakirs, who practise all sorts of imposition to excite the charity of the laity, becoming to appearance maimed, halt, and blind, as seems most calculated to rouse the charitable zeal of admiring enthusiasts, yet I conclude sincere faith does exist; and, where it does, it is found a sufficient incentive to urge men to the self-infliction of the most barbarous penances.

It is said, that a few years since, five Brahmins had been converted to Christianity by some missionaries near Delhi ; but, finding themselves destitute, friendless, and outcast, they solicited permission to be re-admitted to the privileges of their caste. Their prayer was granted, on condition that they performed penance to propitiate their offended deities, by measuring their length to the great temple of D'waka,* visiting the minor temples on their road, and submitting to horrible penances at each. This, the poor creatures willingly agreed to do, and passed through

* Dedicated to Krishna. About six hundred years ago their golden image was stolen, but a new one was placed, which still remains. A pilgrim to D'waka receives from the hands of a Brahmin the stamp of a heated iron instrument, on which is engraved, the shell, the ring, and the lotos flower, which are the insignia of the gods. The average number of pilgrims resorting annually to D'waka has been estimated to exceed fifteen thousand, and the revenue derived to the temple, a lac of rupees.

Bhooj, bruised, emaciated, and way-worn, on their road to the sacred spot assigned for the acceptance of their "work of merit." As these holy places are considered peculiarly favoured by the gods, and all religious ceremonies performed in them efficacious in diverting their anger, they abound in every part of India, and are thronged with devotees. Tanks, rivers, caves, and forests are also considered to be favourite resorts of the deities; and, consequently, various traditions assert them to be fit places whither pilgrimages should be made. But these are of course inferior to the temples, of which those best known are the great temple of Juggernath, and that of Kashee, at Benares. Immediately within reach of the devotees of Cutch is the temple of D'waka, and that of Hinglag in Sindh.* These are both Hindu. The Mahomedan population pay homage at the tombs of their departed saints, whose mausolea they decorate with a curious variety of ornament.

One of these Mahomedan tombs was erected by Rao Lacca, on a rocky eminence overlooking the city of Bhooj, to the memory of a celebrated Mahomedan saint of Bagdat, known as the "Peeran Peer;" another, which is situated near Kaira, has already been noticed. At the tomb of the 'Peeran Peer' is a tree, whose branches, instead of bearing leaves, are thickly covered with

* See "BURNES'S *Travels in Bokharah*.

little bunches of human hair, tied up in bits of various coloured cloths. These are the votive offerings of Mahomedan mothers, who believe that while their children's hair remains near this sacred place, they will be protected from the Evil Eye, disease, and death.

In all these mausolea, the centre of the building immediately below the dome is occupied by a tomb, covered with kinkaub, or richly coloured satin, and at its head an emblazoned Koran, and the supposed turban of the saint; but I believe few of these monuments contain the earthly remains of that departed virtue in whose honour they were erected. The exterior walls are scribbled over with detached sentences from the Koran, repetitions of the holy name, and praises of the deceased. Mendicant and travelling Fakirs, with their bodies smeared with ashes, and crowns of peacock's feathers on their heads, never fail to halt at these places; and, after prostrating themselves at the foot of the tomb, they rise to increase the store in their wallets by the largess of a little flour and a lump of dates, which are provided for the needy, by the charitable contributions of the richer worshippers. Building of tanks, digging of wells, and enclosing of sacred trees are also considered "works of merit;" and it would be well, could the people believe them to be more calculated to procure the final acceptance of their munificent originators, than the erection of temples designed for the performance of fiendish rites, or self-inflicted penances, condemning the victim of them to a life of utter uselessness, or a lingering death of extreme suffering.

The absence of that fear of death, which is so powerful in the hearts of civilized men, is the most remarkable trait in the Hindu character; as a subject of contemplation and enquiry, this has great interest. Probably, the inhabitants of civilized nations set an undue value on life; and this disinclination to shuffle off the "mortal coil" may arise, not alone from those philosophic doubts which puzzle the will, but also from the greater power granted to their imaginations of gathering together the memories of past ages, and indulging those hopes and prospects for the future which they would fain live to see completed. They are not alone content to be; they would desire their being to continue until they see their plans perfected, and their benefits enjoyed; or, perhaps, they would yet tarry, to indulge a little longer in the charms of social life, which so absorb and gratify their spirits. All these feelings are the result of civilization, and of a life made up of the intellectual enjoyments of poetry, painting, books, systems, and leisure. In earlier ages of the world, when the bustle of warlike contention engaged men's energies, and fixed them on external and tangible objects of ambition, life was less esteemed, and often recklessly sacrificed, without a pang, or one care how friends, neighbours, or the old world, would jog on without them. Strong interest, and ever-changing ideas, constitute the value of life ; and where these do not exist, death must seem a desired consummation, to rid us from so tedious, indifferent and joyless a state. Here in part rests the explanation of the indifference to life displayed by the spiritless Hindus. There is no covenant between the world and them that they should cling to its enjoyments ; and their course is a mere succession of animal acts, which, from their very nature, are incapable of giving them any habitual attachment to life. Beyond their present state they believe better things await them ; not those which are pure, holy, and imaginative, but a possession of animal gratification, more intense than mortal strength can sustain ; or a fresh birth in the present world, which shall be free from the pangs now endured. They believe that,

> "All things are but altered, nothing dies,
> And here and there the unbodied spirit flies ;
> By time, or force, or sickness dispossessed,
> And lodges where it lights in man or beast."

Fired by the delirium of this faith, the poor leper flings himself into the flames which he has kindled for his own destruction ; and the decrepit and worn-out sufferer entreats the passer-by to help him into the sacred mud of the Ganges, assured that youth and strength await his approaching change. In these cases a powerful incentive arms the heart against its natural impulses, and elevates the mind beyond their influence. The fatal act once determined on, public opinion defies all interference to prevent its completion, or the suggestion of any ideas but those of hope, merit, and triumph. Far more unaccountable is that constancy of purpose with which these devotees of superstition endure the most exquisite torments, by means of self-inflicted penances, without a sob of anguish. No extent of bodily suffering has sufficient power to make them traitors to their vows, or for a moment to withdraw them from their self-imposed tasks. Physical distortions, the effects of some vow of mutilation, are common, and borne by them with the most unmoved apathy. Swinging from gibbets by means of a rope, and a hook passed through the muscles of the back—running over burning coals—measuring their length on pilgrimages—or rolling around temples, careless of the stones and impediments which lacerate their bodies, — are a few of the tests to which a Hindu devotee subjects himself, to propitiate and prove his devotion to his sanguinary idols.

A wretched fanatic, now in Bombay, took a

little slip of the Tulsi tree, planted it in a pot, placed it in the palm of his left hand, and held it above his head, in which position it has remained for five years. The Tulsi has grown a fine shrub; the muscles of the arm which support it have become rigid and shrunken; the nails of the fingers have grown out, and they curl spirally downwards to a great length; yet the wretched devotee sleeps, eats, drinks, and seems quite indifferent to his strange position, having lost his remembrance of pain in public applause.

Many castes in Cutch* perform what is called Traga, or a self-infliction, which compels the victim's debtor to make good his obligations; or any one to redress an injury he may have committed against him. The form of Traga, in common use, is made by pushing a spear blade through both cheeks, and in this state dancing before the person against whom Traga is made. This is borne on all occasions without a symptom of pain, which if displayed would destroy its efficacy.†

* Principally, however, the Bhats and Charons, or bards and grain merchants.

† Captain Macmurdo states, that the system of Traga was carried to a great length in Cutch some years ago. When plunderers carried off any cattle, the property of the Charons, Bhats, or Brahmins, the whole village would proceed to the spot where the robbers resided; and, in failure of having their property restored, would cut off the heads of several of their

The annals of Hinduism multiply such cases, too painful and harrowing to describe. The devotee

> " Lives not on earth, but in his extasy;
> Around him days and worlds are heedless driven,
> His soul is gone before his dust to heaven."

old men and women, the curse attending these murders falling, not on the murderers, but on the robbers, as the original cause of such an act. Frequent instances occurred, of individuals dressing themselves in cotton quilted cloths steeped in oil, which they set on fire at the bottom, and thus danced before the person against whom Traga was performed, until the miserable creature dropped down and was burnt to ashes. A Cutch chief, during a foray, attempting to escape with his wife and child from a village, was overtaken by his enemy when about to leap a precipice: immediately turning, he cut off his wife's head with his scimitar, and, flourishing his reeking blade in the face of his pursuer, denounced on him the curse of the Traga he had so fearfully performed against him.

CHAPTER XVI.

WORKMEN OF CUTCH.

Phrenological Development of the Organ of Imitation.—Brass-founders, Embroiderers, Armourers, Gold and Silver-smiths, &c.—Cutch Armour.—Matchlocks.—Swords for the Fast of the Mohurrum.—Tambour Embroidery.—Goldsmiths' Imitations of European Patterns.—Talents for Design.—Rudeness of Implements.

WERE the head of a workman of Bhooj to be presented to the observations of Mr. George Combe, he would undoubtedly state the organ of imitation to be its most prominent development. And to this power the natives of Cutch are indebted for much of the fame their beautiful work has acquired, both in England, where it is now well known, and also in all parts of India. The diversity of their talents has classed them as brass-founders, embroiderers, armourers, and cunning workmen in gold and silver. The armour particularly deserves notice, as singularly beautiful in its design, manufacture, and ornament. Every military native of Cutch possesses a sword, shield, and spear, which he is never seen without.

The shield is made of transparent rhinoceros

hide, decorated with gilded wreaths of flowers, and strengthened with bosses of richly-worked Venetian gold.. The spear-handles are made with several joints, of fine steel, brass, and a sort of dead silver, which the workmen plate on iron with surprisingly good effect. In addition to these arms, is the Cutch matchlock; made of unusual length, its dark wood curiously inlaid with ivory and silver. The Cutchee warriors also use that ancient weapon, the axe; the handle of which is beautifully plated with dead silver, inwrought with patterns of graceful foliage in fine gold. Poniards are numerous; some of them of a most exquisite device; the hilts bossed with gems, and the crimson velvet sheaths worked with seed pearls, or a rich filigree pattern of gold or silver. They include also among their weapons the Arab double-edged sword,* which has a slight, straight blade of highly tempered and elastic steel, about six feet long. This tremendous weapon the natives grasp with both hands, and whirl about with the most accomplished ease. During the fast of the Mohurrum, numbers of men, armed with these swords, and a sort of loaded mace much resembling that used by the secutores of the gladiators, precede the ornamented bier of the grandsons of the Prophet; and, when the procession halts, they join in sham

* Better known as Wahabee swords.

combats; a practice which is with these men a sort of authorized profession. In ancient Greece, we are told, it was usual for professional gladiators to exhibit their skill at the funeral ceremonies of the chief consuls, and magistrates of the Republic. The Mahomedans have this custom in common with the Greeks; and it is remarkable that, although the concourse of spectators is immense, and their confusion indescribable, no danger is incurred by the crowd who surround these combatants; their management of the formidable weapons they wield being so eminently skilful.

The embroiderers display much taste in their native designs; but the most remarkable characteristic of their talent is the surprising correctness they display in the art of imitation. They work with a long steel needle, crooked at the point, and, placing the silk below the material to be worked, hook it through, by means of this little implement. They never draw any pattern to guide their stitches, but imitate any embroidery placed before them, by the eye, without even measuring the distances of the pattern. The embroidery is flat, somewhat resembling the old English tambour-work. For working on satins, coloured silks are used; and for velvets, gold thread, spangles, and beads.

The goldsmiths' work of Cutch has been long and justly celebrated. The artizans succeed admirably in imitating European patterns; but the rich purity of the Venetian ore, which they alone use, is seen in greater perfection in the native designs, which are massive, and rich in "barbaric splendour."

The favourite native ornament is the Tulsi, a necklace formed of small plates of richly chased gold, strung on a small wire, or gold thread; ear-rings, also, fastened by a hook which passes through the bore of the ear, and secures them without a clasp; together with a great variety of bangles, or bracelets, usually made of an enormous weight, and adorned with curiously embossed figures of elephants, tigers, snakes, and monkeys. In common with the armourers, the goldsmiths work gold ornaments on a pure dead silver ground, with great taste and delicacy of design. This description of work is principally in favour for sherbet bowls, and golaubdanis, or rose-water sprinklers; the elegant forms for which are copied from those made in opal and china, which are brought from Turkey, as articles of merchandise with Persia.

The goldsmiths design remarkably well, and both draw and colour their designs with great correctness. In total ignorance of Hogarth's line of beauty, their acquaintance with the peculiar curve which constitutes grace in all delineations of the fine arts, is every where developed; and few models of ancient art can display forms more elegant than the Hindus choose for their common water vessels, the designs for their embroidery, the garlands and wreaths which every where adorn their temples, tombs, and palaces.

The workmen have few tools, and those they have are of the most primitive description. Thus, in embossing a cup, or snuff-box, which when finished displays a graceful garlanding of the most delicate flowers, with minute leaves, tendrils, and stems connecting them, the workman forms a large lump of lac round a wooden handle in the form desired, and, having moulded the silver on it, punches it out, in the pattern he requires it to be, by means of a little rough awl, apparently more calculated to mar, than to perfect, the tasteful elegance of the artist's design. The execution of work under these disadvantages is necessarily tedious ; but its exactness and beauty must proportionably raise our admiration of the manual dexterity of the native artisan.

CHAPTER XVII.

MINSTRELSY OF CUTCH.

National Melodies. — Hindu Musical Rhythm. — Knowledge of the Arts a Revelation from Heaven. — The Indian Apollo, the First Musician. — Cupid led Captive by Apollo.—Hindu Diatonic Scale. —Musical Notation.—Untranslated Collection of Poems in Sanskreet.—Instrumental Music. — The Vina. — The Pukhawuj. — The Sitarr, or Guitar.—The Saringi, or Fiddle. — Wandering Minstrels. —Probable Origiu of the Gypsies.

As connected with the early history of an uncivilized people, few researches are so curious and interesting in their nature, as an inquiry into the degree of knowledge they may have possessed of the fine arts. Being durable in many of their productions, and acquired by oral communication, the arts frequently afford, to the philosophical examiner of social improvement, his only *data*, in a history of progress. Of the imitative arts, music, as the offspring of the most simple and pastoral times, will, perhaps, be found on the earliest record. It is not difficult to believe, that the first principles of melody, which, by the aid of mathematics and physics, have led to the formation of an abstruse and complicated science, had for their origin the simple strains of some shepherd boy; who, feeding his flocks on the solitary mountains of the East, broke a fragment from the springing reed, and beguiled his lonely hours by an attempted imitation of the sounds around him.

Every country possesses a style of melody peculiarly its own; and as this national expression probably results from the habitual passions and affections of its people, the study of such peculiarities becomes useful, as an index to their moral and social condition.

In common with the ancient Greeks, but, perhaps, anterior to them, the Hindus proved their acquaintance with musical rhythm, both as an art capable of exciting the strongest passions, and as productive of the most pleasurable ideas. Many learned treatises are to be found, amongst old Hindu writings, on the subject of musical composition; and the authors hesitate not to ascribe to the practice of this enchanting art, the most astonishing effects. Antelopes, we are told, have been charmed by it to the dens of savage beasts; the most venomous snakes have been lured from their holes; and nightingales, vainly endeavouring to vie with the musician, are alleged to have dropped from the trees in an extasy of enjoyment.

The Hindus also believe that all knowledge of

the arts is a revelation from heaven. Their musical treatises are written in a peculiar character, called the language of the gods; and their deities are supposed to have been the early practisers of the rules they contain. Thus, their sacred books record many graceful tales of the Indian Apollo, who, touching his lute in pastoral roundelays near the silver waters of the Jumna,* is said to have so filled the air with its ravishing sweetness, that the waters ceased to flow, the flocks and herds abandoned their pastures, bands of youthful shepherds and smiling damsels followed him entranced; whilst Camdeo,† himself led captive, compelled all nature to confess the mingled power of melody and love.

To express the idea of music, the Hindus use the word Sangita, which means literally a concert; and not only a harmonic arrangement of sweet sounds, but as combining the charms of melody, poetry, and motion; or, as an elegant oriental scholar has remarked, "three beautiful arts, like

* The river Jumna, near Delhi; described as a spot rendered most lovely, by the unusual beauty of its sylvan scenery, and celebrated as the favourite resort of Krishna. In ancient times, the science of music was carried to a high degree of excellence at Delhi; and, according to historic record, the Emperor Mahomed Shah sacrificed his throne to its enchantments.

† The Indian Cupid.

the graces united in a dance," together captivate and charm the sense.*

The musical modes of the Hindus are extremely curious; and although it is not my intention to enter fully into a subject so complicated and abstruse, a succinct account of their principal divisions may not be deemed uninteresting.

The Hindu musicians have a diatonic scale of seven primitive notes, agreeing in sound, I believe, with our major mode. These notes are arranged into six simple melodies, entitled Rawgs, or modes; and these are again variated into thirty-six airs, or branches, called Rawgnees. The six Rawgs, and the Rawgnees, are supposed to have an imaginary existence, as nymphs and genii, and to preside over the divisions of time. The six Rawgs answer to the morning, noon, sunset, evening, midnight, and dawn; and the thirty-six Rawgnees attend the intermediate hours. They have also six airs for the seasons, which are considered as the offspring of the Rawgnees, and are more modern compositions. All the Hindu songs are written for these airs; and it is considered

* According to Sir William Jones, the Indian treatises on music describe the Sangita as consisting of three parts; or song, percussion, and dancing: the first comprises poetry, the second instrumental music, and the third theatrical representation.

bad taste to play them at any but their appointed hours.

I have not been able to find that the Hindus possess any system of musical notation. Their modes are acquired orally; and they possess books called the Rawg-malas, which contain songs adapted to the thirty-six airs, but without musical notes. All the songs in these books are headed with paintings of the nymphs and genii of the Hindu modes, each bearing the title of a Rawg-nee.*

Every branch of knowledge amongst the Hindus, however scientific may be its subject, is embellished with beautiful allegories, and poetical ideas; and in their musical divisions, this is most remarkable. Not only are the six Rawgs themselves described as six genii, wedded to nymphs beautiful as Houris, but we are assured that these airs are the favorite melodies of flights of fairies, who sing to them the loves of Krishna and Radha, at the banquets of the heaven-born Indra.†

* The word Mala literally signifies a string, and in the title of this work is united with Rawg, to signify the succession of airs, in these peculiar modes.

† A small collection of poems in Sanskreet, entitled the "Subhaw Bilaus, or Ornament of Society, a work at present untranslated, contains the names of all the Rawgs and Rawgnees, with directions for their personification in the Rawg-malas. The names of the Rawgs, and the times at which they

The musicians of Cutch are acquainted with all these principles of composition, and have attained considerable proficiency in their application.

They use instrumental music for three purposes: as an assistance of bardic recitals; as an accompaniment to the movements of their dancers; and as forming a part of their religious ceremonies.

The most favorite instrument in use is the Bin, or Vina. It has a finger-board resembling that of the guitar, supported on two large gourds, one at each end. The manner of playing on it is, to allow one gourd to rest on the knee, and the other at the back of the shoulder: the frets are unusually high and broad; and the strings, being of brass and iron wire, the instrument would seem

are appointed to be sung, are as follows: Bhairo, for the morning; Deepuck, for noon; Shreerawg, for sunset; Hindola, for evening; Soohnee, for midnight; and Maulkose, for the dawn. To these airs the most wonderful effects are assigned: amongst others, the author asserts, that the air Deepuck, when properly played, will cause a lamp or candle to ignite. An air called Migrawg, is appointed to be sung during rain.

Some of the Rawg-malas are very delicately and correctly pencilled, and would be considered curious as works of art. Each air is represented by the delineation of a nymph or genius, holding a lotus flower, or a Vina, and reclining under the shade of a lofty tree. Over the figure, is written the name of the Rawg, or Rawgnee, and below it, an ode, suited to that particular air.

peculiarly difficult to use; the more so, as the character of the music played requires considerable execution. The fingers of the right hand, however, are armed with wire shields, and the left hand supports the instrument. The Vina has seven wires; but although the Greeks believed, that the seven strings of Apollo's harp were the symbolical representations of the seven planets, I am not aware that the wires of the Vina involve any graceful allegory.

The Rawgnees are usually played upon the Vina, accompanied by the Pukhawuj, a small drum used for the purpose of keeping time. All these airs are distinguished by a poetic name, but the sameness of them is remarkable. The most pleasing air I have heard is the "midnight" Rawg; it is a sweet and simple melody, but generally encumbered by the artist with variations of unimaginable tediousness. A Hindu musician uses his gamut, like the figures of a Chinese puzzle, or the beads of a kaliedoscope, shifting them into the most singular positions, yet every change bearing a most fraternal resemblance to the rest. A transition is seldom made from the original key, although they possess a great variety of modes; and their skill seems to be displayed in the exercise of peculiar ingenuity. A native musician will remain engaged in a display of his art, for many hours, apparently without fatigue, delighting his audience, but wearing himself a countenance of the most intense anxiety.

In addition to the Vina, the Cutch minstrels use the Sitarr, or guitar, the Saringi, or fiddle, the Rubbab, or lyre, and the Murchung, a sort of jews' harp. All these instruments are accompanied by either small drums of various tones, or cymbals, to keep measures, and accent the airs.

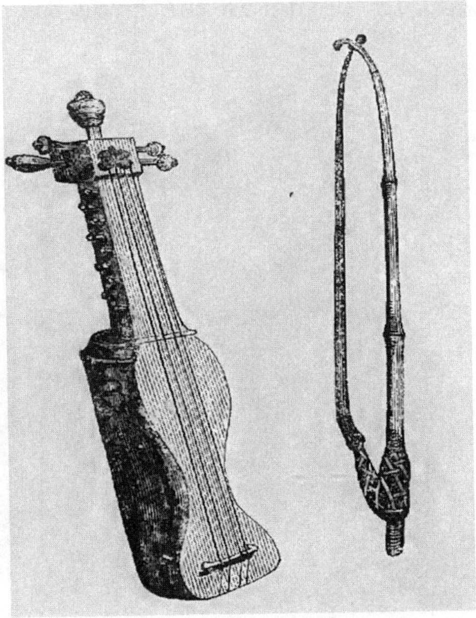

The bowls of all these instruments are made from gourds, and are strung with wire. The prejudices of the Hindus forbid the use of animal fibre ; consequently, the Brahmins, who condescend to practise these instruments, would consider their sacred fingers defiled by the touch of a cat-gut string.

In their temples they allow only drums and cymbals to be used; the din of which is sometimes increased beyond its common intensity by the addition of the Sanooree, a rude horn possessing great shrillness. Itinerant musicians are sometimes to be met in the large towns of Anjar,

Mandavie, and Bhooj. They are usually of the Kalatnee caste, and travel together in small parties; the men carry the Sitarr, and a gourd containing a few trifles, or a little grain for their support; whilst the women who accompany them chaunt a wild, but plaintive melody, pleasing to the ear from its extreme simplicity.

The Kalatnees are a low-caste race, very poor, but abundantly cunning, and ingenious in their calling. They are a vagrant tribe, and gain a living by the arts of juggling and minstrelsy. Some modern writer considers them synonymous with the Mahratta Vanjari, from whom is traced the probable origin of the gypsies.

Few of the natives study music as an art; and the practice of it is restricted chiefly to hired minstrels. Wealthy persons generally retain such men; and the poor are content with the strains of wandering minstrels, and the sonorous clamour of their religious worship. Women of character never practise any branch of the fine arts, as it is considered incompatible with morality and good breeding.

In conclusion, I must offer the opinion, that although Hindu music, as played in Cutch, has little variety of subject, yet their instrumental performances are pleasing, from their perfect correctness in time and tune.

* See GRELLMAN, *On the Origin of Gypsies.*

CHAPTER XVIII.

ON THE BARDS AND BARDIC LITERATURE OF CUTCH.

Talent for Narration in Barbarous Times. — Story-tellers. — Hindu Romances, and Persian Poetry.—Poetical Description of Krishna. —Bhats and Dadies, Provincial Bards of Cutch.—Composition of Metrical Ballads.—Marriage Festivals. — History of the Birth of Lacka Phoolanee, or the Flower of the Sun.—Original Cutchee Ode in Praise of Lacka Phoolanee.—A Secret, valuable as that of the Philosopher's Stone. — Romantic History of Two Lovers, Soosie and Punoon.—Rules for Persian Versification.—Examples.—Hafiz. —Romance of the Marriage of Love and Beauty.—Persian Fables. —The Rose and the Grass. — The Man, the Snake, and the Fox; a Tale, translated from the Anwari Soheili of Kashifi. — Credulity of the Cutch Bhats.

The talent for narration seems essentially the art of barbarous times. In all ages, story-tellers have been held in high estimation by nations whose literature was limited, whose tastes afforded them few amusements, and whose resources were confined to hunting, to the practice of arms, and to the relations of their household bards.

The taste appears to have been independent of climate, and to have arisen as much from the mental necessities and warlike spirit of men, as from a state of physical indolence, induced by a high degree of temperature. Thus the Sagas, or ancient poems of Iceland, were the progenitors of those well known Norman ballads, which are said to have inflamed the martial spirit of half Europe; whilst the bardic remains of the Celts and other northern people afford most interesting glimpses into the condition and military enthusiasm of times too barbarous to have left us any other chronicle. So late even as the sixteenth century, bards and domestic story-tellers seem to have formed part of all wealthy establishments, in Ireland, Scotland, and Wales; but as civilization advanced, this class of retainers disappeared, and it is to be regretted that so few of their productions have been preserved which can be depended on as genuine specimens of bardic style.

Italy still boasts of her *improvisatori;* but they also have lost much of their reputation for genius since the days of Boccaccio and Ariosto; and in the East alone, remains that combination of physical temperament with exuberance of fancy, which has long tended to foster an unwearying taste for bardic literature.

A disposition, so characteristic of orientals, may readily be traced to the effects of climate, in forming the social manners of the people, who, indolent by nature, unacquainted with general literature, and unused to female society, are addicted to the constant use of opium or a hookah, and find their principal delight in sitting for hours, inhaling the perfume of garakoe, whilst their senses are lulled, or their imaginations diverted, by the ingenious relations of their bards and story-tellers.

Wealthy natives usually entertain some domestic Feramorz, who thus whiles away the tedium of their listless hours with Hindu romances, and even draws from the rich treasury of Persian poesy thrilling tales of the loves of Leila* and Mujnoon, to add their captivations to the glowing couplets of Hafiz and Jayadeva.† All classes of natives sympathise in this taste, and multiply legends of their gods and sages. The sacred books, and most particularly the Puranas, abound with fabulous histories of the Hindu deities, many

* The Petrarch and Laura of the East.

† Containing the loves of Heri, the pastoral name for Krishna. The following is a description of Krishna, as extracted from the songs of Jayadeva, the great lyric poet of the Hindus. "His azure breast glittered with pearls of unblemished lustre, like the full bed of the cerulean Yamuna (Jumna) interspersed with curls of white foam. From his graceful waist flowed a pale yellow robe, which resembled the golden dust of the water lily, scattered over its blue petals. His eyes played like a pair of water birds with azure plumage, that sport near a full-blown lotos, on a pool in the season of dew. Bright ear-rings, like two suns, displayed in full ex-

of them graceful and pleasing, but the majority coarse and licentious in the extreme.

The fountain head of Paganism was ever to be found in Asia; and the classic and poetic Greeks, even in those early ages when Plutarch tells us "their all monstrous and tragical land" was occupied only by poets and fabulists, yet knew little, compared with the Hindu writers, of that deep spirit of allegory which enwraps all their allusions to the acts and to the nature of their deities. The Song of Solomon, perhaps, may convey some idea of their style; but even that masterpiece of Israelitish allegory reaches not the depths of Hindu mysticism. The Brahmins, learned in these histories, diffuse them amongst the people as traditions; and the most ridiculous tales of Krishna and Radha are repeated, as a Scotch gude wife would relate a legend of the brownies to her fire-side gossips. The Persian tales are very superior to these, being less marvellous, but more ingenious and graceful in their

pansion the flowers of his cheeks and lips, which glistened with the liquid radiance of smiles. His locks, interwoven with blossoms, were like a cloud variegated with moon-beams; and on his forehead shone a circle of odorous oil, extracted from the sandal of Malaya, like the moon just appearing on the dusky horizon, while his whole body seemed in a flame from the blaze of unnumbered gems." *Asiatic Researches*, vol. iii.

incidents, and holding in solution, as it were, a greater proportion of morality. The best known of them are contained in the Gulistan of Sady; but the Eight Gates of the verdant garden* share admiration with the richly gemmed odes of Anacreontic Hafiz, whose love-inspiring couplets are usually selected to accompany the Natch; a dance which has been frequently and minutely described.

As provincial bards, Cutch possesses its Bhats and Dadies, whose profession it is to rehearse to the Jharrejah chiefs the warlike deeds of their ancestry, whose glory is thus embalmed in the exaggerated metaphor of ancient story, originally composed to exalt the fame of the warrior princes, and draw down a shower of their choicest favours. We were favoured with a visit from a celebrated Jharrejah bard, well learned in the early history of Cutch; he brought with him a volume of manuscript odes, written in the Guzzerati dialect, the sole topic of which was royal panegyric. At our request, he sang several of them to his Sitarr, with a pleasing and melodious voice, and in conclusion afforded me an interesting explanation of his art.

It is curious to remark the intelligence possessed by these bards, who are really proficient in the art they practise. The metrical ballads of

* Alluding to the division of subjects in the Gulistan.

Cutch are composed in twenty-four different descriptions of verse, all of which are in common use amongst the provincial bards. These rules are acquired orally; and, with the exception of the Jharrejah Bhats, which are written in the Cutchee dialect, by means of the Guzzerati character, all their local odes and tales are communicated *viva voce.* The immense collection of songs and stories, so retailed, forms a very remarkable instance of the power of practice, in developing the strength of memory, even when the fancy and understanding have had little share in the impression. All these bards are acquainted with from three to four hundred stories, odes, and songs each, composed either on incidents of their early local history, or on supposed and very marvellous interpositions of the Hindu deities in trivial mundane affairs.

On the celebration of marriages and other festivals, the Bhats attend, and *improvise* epithalamiums, and various odes, for which they receive a slight remuneration. Amongst the practisers of the bardic art, a distinction exists, which, perhaps, is not much regarded by inferior artists, although founded on priestly prejudice. It is between the castes of Bhats and Dadies, both of them being local bards, but distinguishable by minor peculiarities. A Bhat signifies a relater of songs and stories, and a chaunter of local odes in praise of the Jharrejah chiefs and Rajpoot princes of

Cutch; known as Bhats, from the title of the men who sing them.* Many of these bards are Brahmins; and, by reason of the prejudices of their calling, are accustomed both to sing and *raconte* without accompaniment. The Dadie is also a vocalist and a story-teller; and, in addition to this, he is the leader of a little instrumental band, who assist him by an accompaniment to his vina, and by the introduction of symphonies, as he wearies in his relation. The stories he chaunts are usually in a kind of rude and simple verse; but if in prose, the Dadie succeeds in ekeing out a measured cadence by the varied intonation of his voice; and it is curious to observe, how perfectly use has trained these men to economise their breath, and for how long a period, and with what rapid enunciation, they can continue their narrations.

The Bhats and odes being all in the Cutchee language, it is impossible to do justice to them by translation, or to convey an idea of local manners so exact as may be required to render them intelligible. The possession, however, of an art of poetry by so rude a people may be considered

* Bhát, or Bhăt, is derived from the Sanskreet Bártà, signifying a word. There are three descriptions of Bhats in India: the historians, the genealogists, and they whose duty it is to salute, early in the morning, the Rajah or chief, and, in well chosen phrases, to wish him health, long life, and prosperity.

interesting to the curious in such matters; and I will, therefore, subjoin for their amusement a few literal translations of these primitive compositions, which may enable the reader to judge both of their peculiar style, and the degree of merit they possess.

The following Bhat contains the "History of the Birth of Lacka-phoolanee, or the Flower of the Sun," a celebrated Rajpoot prince, who is said to have reigned at Kairah in this province about nine hundred years ago.

"As the beautiful Somel Upsura was wandering in the rose-gardens of the Zenana, during the absence of her lord, the Sun, beholding her charms, was pierced with the arrows of love, and dropped at her feet a lotos flower, as the messenger of his desires. The fair Somel yielded to her divine lover, and the nectar-laden gale echoed back her sighs. As her husband approached, her beautiful face was darkened with grief, and sadness rested in her eyes. She confessed her condition, and entreated death from his hand; but her loveliness prevailed; he meditated only on his unknown rival, and hastened to destroy the fruit of her inconstancy. Preparing a cup of water with poisonous gums, he raised it to her lips, when the bright-haired god burst through the vernal clouds, and declared the divine origin of the child, who was born, and named the "Flower of the Sun," whom all the heavenly maids caressed, and all the gods received with acclamations and delight."

The following Ode in Praise of Lacka-phoolanee I have given in the original Cutchee, to afford a specimen of the peculiar sort of verse used in these compositions.

LACKA-PHOOLANEE.

Prusm wurs puchwees pat bieto pat o dur
Mungul dummul pirj milee kunuk foolie foolie dur
Wullee wurs puchas phirio Kutuki Pholanee
Mao kund tanar nir nimae an phiree apanee
Jae surj sukat Lako jus baro lio
Puchwees wurs doonah puchee Kot Raj Karah Rio
Sehees ek samut boop dus lak bunejie
Weparee punj lak lak bat charon bhae
Katur ud lak lak neesan bujae
Beeju nirunt beeha soojee nuheen
Pundur phir jojun puree choud Kror purgo numunt.
Tudeo "Puhoo Pasar" Lako churee.*

TRANSLATION.

Lacka Phoolanee was twenty-five years old when he on the throne became king.

Dancing, and rejoicing amongst much people, the world blossomed like gold.

* In the original Cutch character, this metre is governed by the number of letters which compose each line, without being restricted to any particular number of metrical feet.

After twenty-five years, with a large force, Pholanee made excursions;
The nine divisions of the earth he conquered, and his order was absolute.
After another twenty-five, he established his Raj at Kaira;
Seventeen lacs of Zemindars, a krore of nobles,
A thousand heroes, ten thousand great men,
Five lacs of merchants, one lac of story-tellers,
Half a lac of cultivators, beaters of royal drums one lac;
Of other people beyond calculation.
Fifteen jojuns,* the circuit of his army, fourteen krores of salaams,
When Lacka mounted his horse, Puhoo Pasar!

All the people in Cutch believe in the possibility of obtaining eternal youth and unwasting riches, by means of the "waters of life" and the "philosopher's stone;" and many Indian works contain grave treatises on the best means for seeking them. It is hardly necessary to add, that none but devotees need attempt it. The following Bhat tells us of a mighty king, who, if he lacked the philosopher's stone, discovered a secret quite as valuable.

BHAT.

"It is related, that during the reign of a king of Cutch, named Lakeh, a Jogie† lived, who was

* A jojun is four coss; a coss being two English miles.

† Fakir, or holy man.

a wise man, and wonderfully skilled in the properties of herbs. For years he had been occupied in searching for a peculiar kind of grass, the roots of which should be burnt, and a man be thrown into the flames. The body so burnt would become gold, and any of the members might be removed, without the body sustaining any loss ; as the parts so taken would always be self-restored.

"It so occurred, that this Jogie, whilst following a flock of goats, observed one amongst them eating of the grass he was so anxious to procure. He immediately rooted it up, and desired the shepherd who was near to assist him in procuring fire-wood. When he had collected the wood, and kindled a flame, into which the grass was thrown, the Jogie, wishing to render the shepherd the victim of his avarice, desired him, under some pretence, to make a few circuits round the fire. The man, however, suspecting foul play, watched his opportunity, and, seizing the Jogie himself, he threw him into the fire and left him to be consumed. Next day, on returning to the spot, great was his surprise to behold the golden figure of a man lying amongst the embers. He immediately chopped off one of the limbs and hid it. The next day he returned to take another, when his astonishment was yet greater to see that a fresh limb had replaced the one already taken. In short, the shepherd soon became wealthy, and revealed the secret of his riches to the king, Lakeh, who, by the same means, accumulated so much gold, that every day he was in the habit of giving one lac and twenty-five thousand rupees in alms to fakirs."

Another very favourite tale, related as a Bhat, both in Cutch and Sindh, is the romantic history of two lovers named "Soosie and Punoon;" and is as follows.

"In the city of Burhamanabad, resided a rich man, whose wife, after remaining many years childless, brought forth a daughter. The father's happiness was complete; but, on consulting the astrologers, they predicted, that the child would marry a Mahomedan. To avoid so disgraceful a connection, the father determined to destroy his daughter, and for this purpose placed the child in a basket, and threw it into the river. By chance, the basket floated to the city of Burumpore, and was picked up by a man in the employ of a Dhobie* of that place, who took it to his master. He, finding the child alive, and being himself childless, immediately adopted it. In time, Soosie, as they called the little damsel, became so celebrated for her beauty, that whenever she went abroad her footsteps were followed by all the people of the city.

* Washerman.

"It happened, that a caravan of merchants halted at Burumpore, and some of them having seen the girl, on their return reported her beauty to Punoon, the son of the governor of Cutch. He became enamoured of the description, and, disguising himself as a merchant, travelled with the next caravan, for the purpose of satisfying himself as to the truth of the reports respecting Soosie. The better to carry his design into execution, he entered into the service of the Dhobie, and was soon convinced that the real charms of the maiden exceeded all description. In a short time he acquainted her with his passion, which she returned, and, by the consent of the Dhobie, they were married.

"When this intelligence reached Punoon's father, he, annoyed at such a connection, dispatched two of his sons to bring Punoon home. Arrived at Burumpore, the brothers took up their residence near the Dhobie's house; and, watching for an opportunity, they one night seized Punoon, and, placing him on a swift camel, returned with him to their father.

"The grief of Soosie, on hearing of the abduction of her husband, knew no bounds. She determined to follow him, and took the road to Cutch. After travelling about forty coss,* overcome with thirst and fatigue, she fell exhausted to

* A coss is about two miles.

the ground; but as she fell, her foot struck a stone, and immediately there gushed forth a stream of limpid water, with which she became refreshed. This spring yet remains, nor was it ever known to fail, even in seasons when all other springs, wells, and tanks have been dried up. Soosie, in remembrance of the goodness of God, planted, on the edge of the spring, a sprig of that tree from which henna is procured; and the shrub is to be seen there at the present day.*

"Proceeding on towards the hills, fatigue and and thirst again assailed her, and in addition to her griefs a shepherd, observing her desolate condition, and being struck with her fairy-like beauty, advanced for the purpose of offering her insult and violence. Soosie, however, by reiterated entreaties, softened his nature, and induced him to desist from his wicked design, until he should have provided her with means wherewith to satisfy her parching thirst. Whilst the shepherd departed to procure her some milk, Soosie prayed to be released from her many calamities. Her supplications were heard: the hill whereon she stood opened; she fearlessly entered the fissure; and the hill closed on her, leaving nothing visible but the edge of her Saree. When the shepherd returned, he reproached himself bitterly, as the cause of this calamity, and piled a few stones together as a me-

* The "Mendee," or *Lamsonia inermis.*

morial of his grief. Meanwhile, Punoon continued inconsolable at the separation from his beloved wife; and his father, seeing that he was determined rather to die than live without her, dispatched him in charge of his brothers to seek Soosie. When they arrived on the hills, and were informed by the shepherd, who still lingered on the spot of her miraculous disappearance, they were overwhelmed with astonishment and grief. Punoon, however, under the pretence of offering up his devotions at the temporary monument erected over his wife by the shepherd, fervently prayed, that God, even in death, would join him to his beloved Soosie. His petition was heard; the hill side again opened; and where the last flutterings of her Saree had been seen, the beautiful Soosie was rejoined by her adored Punoon."

These stories, which were related to me by Bhats in the language of Cutch, afford a fair specimen of their favourite styles of composition; but, as the warlike spirit of the people has become less energetic, from the influence of political circumstances, the Bhats in praise of their Jharejah chiefs are less frequently related, and love tales and fables are listened to with greater interest.

In addition to provincial poets, bards from Hindustan are retained in Cutch by the Rao and other great men; those bards having, by means of oral communication, become acquainted with many of the ingenious fables and graceful love stories to be found in Persian and Sanskreet literature. As these are becoming rapidly engrafted on the more simple and national productions of Cutch, it is probable that, after a few more years of peace, little vestige will remain of the original Bhats, which are at least curious, as the genuine compositions of an unlettered and simple people.

Without any intention of writing an essay on either Persian poetry or prose, it may afford some amusement to those who are unacquainted with the literature of the East, to give a brief account of the rules for Persian versification, and a few specimens of the style of their favourite authors.

The Persian rules of versification are singularly severe, and would appear materially calculated to repress the impulses of genius in their poets, even without referring to a state of social error, which in Persia has long continued to check all development of the social affections. This, in restricting her authors to a paucity of topics, has caused a sameness and monotony of subject in all their compositions, for which the sweetest versification cannot atone.

The Persian poets possess eight different descriptions of verse, all of which are restricted within a given number of couplets, or lines. These measures are selected by the poets, according to the subject of their poems.

The most peculiar of their compositions is the ghazel; a form peculiar to Persia, and selected by Hafiz as the measure in which the greater number of his charming odes are written. The following is a specimen of this style, as translated by the elegant pen of Colonel Kennedy:—

GHAZEL.

I.

While here reclined that cheek's bright rose to me 's enough:
Far be from me the men who feign devotion's zeal;
For virtuous deeds be paradise the blest reward;
Beside the streamlet seated, mark how life glides on:
Behold this world's delights, and view its various pains:
Why seek another joy when here my love reclines?
Not e'en to Paradise I'd fly, did God permit:
Why, Hafiz, then condemn the lot to each assigned?

II.

The shade that Cypress here bestows to me 's enough.
The joy that from the goblet flows to me 's enough.
The cell where Pagans wine expose to me 's enough.
That sign how swift each moment goes to me 's enough.
If not to you, the joy it shows to me 's enough.
The bliss her converse fond bestows to me 's enough;
Love sweeter far than angel knows to me 's enough.
A guileless heart with verse that glows to me 's enough.

The ghazel ought not to consist of less than

five, or more than twelve couplets. The verses of the first couplet rhyme together: the verses of the other couplets do not; and again, each couplet ends with the same rhyme as the first. It will be observed, also, that to the regular rhyme which concludes the couplets, an addition is made of three words—"to me's enough." This is remarkable in many of the odes of Hafiz; and although monotonous perhaps to a European ear, is considered harmonious and beautiful by the Persians.

The following is a literal translation of a ghazel, composed by Hafiz in the same measure as the foregoing, and may form material for practice in Persian versification.

GHAZEL.

This garment which I have, *it were better* to mortgage in a wine shop.

And this record of insignificance, *it were better* to drown in wine.

When I had wasted my days with looking into all things, I found *it were better* to lie down in the corner of dissipation.

The secrets of the hypocritical bigot I will not divulge to the people, for this is a story *it were better* to recite before the harp and lute.

I will not alienate myself from a mistress like you; if I deserve torture, *it were better* to be tortured by thy waving tresses.

Oh Hafiz! when you become old, frequent not drinking-houses, wandering and dissipation, *it were better* to practise in youth.

In this ghazel, it will be observed that the close of each couplet must be the words, "it were better," as they are translated according to the original.

The following literal translation is of an ode which is composed of simple ryhming couplets, corresponding to those known in England, and without this peculiarity.

ODE.

Many crowned heads are slaves to thine infecting eyes, and many, famed for wisdom, become inebriated by thy rosy lips.

The zephyrs and my tears are informers against us, but lovers do not divulge their own secrets.

When, oh zephyr! thou passest through the waving locks of my beloved, observe to thy right and left how many lovers are tormented.

We are predestined for paradise; therefore depart, O holy man! for sinners are most entitled to forgiveness. It is not I alone who recite verses on thy rosy cheeks, thou hast a thousand nightingales on every side, who sing thy praise.

Go to the wine bowers, and dye thy cheeks with red, but go not to the temple, to feign devotion's zeal.

Hafiz does not pray to be loosed from the bondage of thy musk-shedding locks, for they who are bound by thy shining tresses are most free.

The only topics of Hafiz are the raptures of love and wine, a few reflections on the transitoriness of the world, and the praises of his mistress. The poet introduces his name into all the concluding couplets; and as this is customary, the Persian poets choose particular appellations, suitable to the harmony of verse. The real name of Hafiz was Shamsud Din Muhammad; and Niamut Khan, the favourite wit and poet of Alumgeer, adopted the poetic name of Aalee.

The other classifications of Persian verse are into Kasidehs, Quatahs, Rabacs, Mosallas, Mokammas, and Masnavis; the last of which are simply rhyming couplets, consisting of verses in nine, ten, or eleven syllables.

The Biet consists of only two lines, and the Misrah of one. Of these trifling compositions the following are translations:—

BIET.

Oh! Hafiz, the time of separation has ended, and I perceive the altar-scented form of my love;
Oh! distressed lover, rejoice and be gay, on this happy occasion.

MISRAH.

Come! and from our hearts remove these hills of grief.

The Persian poets are peculiarly remarkable for their abundant metaphor, which, originating perhaps in defect of language, may sometimes render the style of their prose writings obscure; but undoubtedly it adds much to the delicacy, sweetness, and harmony of their poetical compositions.

Amongst the works of the poet Aalee, is a most graceful and charming romance, entitled "The Marriage of Love and Beauty." It is, I believe, untranslated, and forms part of a small volume written on the wars of Alumgeer, in rare Persian, rendered even more than usually obscure by the introduction of Sanskreet idioms.

The outline of the tale is as follows.

ROMANCE OF THE MARRIAGE OF LOVE AND BEAUTY.

"Love, who is the offspring of Madness, coming of age, dispatches a messenger called Sight of the Eyes, to seek for him a wife. Sight of the Eyes speedily meets Beauty, sporting in the meadows of Fancy, and woos her to become the Bride of Love. Beauty, after consulting with her parents, Dignity and Sweetness, and with her guardian, Discretion, consents, and Joy departs with the news. When the marriage-day arrives, Love and Beauty proceed towards the temple of Possession. Beauty is arrayed in the ear-rings of secresy, the necklace of Modesty, and the bangles of Agitation. She is attended by her nymphs, Fair-colour, Ruby-lips, and Soft-heart; and followed by the Genii of Exaction, Ill-temper, and Conceit, who bear a dowry of restlessness and sighs to bestow upon Love, who meets her, attended by his followers, Jealousy, Hope, Tenderness, and Desire. Affection, hand in hand with Admiration, departs to seek a Moolah; but the Moolah declines to unite the pair, on the ground of the union being a worldly one. In this dilemma, Eagerness and Inclination set forth, and return with an old Cazi, called Mutual Agreement, who solemnises the compact, and concludes by declaring that the happy couple shall enjoy eternal youth, that Beauty shall be always attended by Love, and Love shall never cease to be attracted by the musk-shedding tresses of Beauty."

This is of course only a mere sketch of the machinery of the tale, which is beautifully heightened and developed by the most graceful metaphors. The author, who was a wit as well as a poet, preserved his appointment as the favourite officer and companion of the emperor, entirely from his remarkable talent. Alumgeer was a bigotted Soonee, and Niamut Khan as bigotted a Sheeah, but the prince could not consent to allow a religious difference to deprive him of the gem of his court.

The frequent use of tropes by the Persian writers affords strength and conciseness to their style, but they are not so generally used with reference to this effect, as they are with the object of rousing the fancy, and diverting the mind with combinations of ideas independent of the immediate incidents of a story.

The most curious part of Persian literature are its fables, which are highly esteemed as didactic writings amongst the Persians, and have also been appreciated all over Europe, by means of imitations and translations. Prosopopœia, or personification, is a favourite figure in all oriental writings; and in didactic works especially is used to convey every variety of moral sentiment. Our social sympathies are constantly excited for trees, rivers, snakes, &c.; and although, as a learned writer has observed, there is an inattention to propriety in introducing a devout tiger, or an old mouse well read in the Shastrus, this style of writing affords their moral authors the opportunity of introducing, in their fabulous tales, a greater number of political maxims and social satires, than might be well received by their countrymen, if attired in any other garb. The Persians neither practise nor understand morality; yet their works breathe the most pure and delicate sentiments, and few people descant so energetically on the distinctions of virtue and vice. In prose, their most admired works on moral subjects are, the Gulistan of Sadi, and the Anwari Soheili of Kashifi. The first of these has been frequently noticed, but I cannot resist transcribing one tale from Mr. Gladwin's translation. Its commencement would form admirable couplets, to interweave, in the oriental style, with Lawrence Sterne's admirable sermon, on "Trust in God." Sadi has displayed in its tone all Sterne's tenderness and benevolence, but has introduced his moral with a majesty of sweetness which our Yorick can never rival.

TALE XLVIII.

"I saw some nosegays of fresh roses tied to a dome with some grass. I said, 'What is this worthless grass, that it should be in the company of roses?' The grass wept, and said, 'Be silent; the benevolent forget not their associates. Although I have neither beauty, nor colour, nor odour, still, am not I the grass of God's garden? I am the servant of the munificent God, nourished from of old by his bounty; whether I possess virtue or not, I look for the mercy of God. Although I have not any worth, neither possess the means of shewing my obedience, he is able to save his servant, although destitute of all other support.' It is the custom that masters should liberate their old slaves. O God! who hast ornamented this world with thy creatures, bestow liberty on this thine old servant. O Sadi! pursue the road to the temple of resignation. O man of God! walk in the path of righteousness. Unfortunate is that person who turns his head from this gate, since he will not be able to find another."

The Anwari Soheili is a collection of tales and fables interspersed with moral couplets and reflections. Many of these are pleasing, yet they introduce so much which is foreign to the immediate sentiment of the composition, that they frequently become tedious, as episodes usually are, when intruded into a well-told tale. The following is a specimen of this style of composition, translated from the work in question. The original is more free from these defects than many similar productions of the same author; but even in this instance, I have found it necessary to obey the injunctions said to have been given by the Emperor Akbar to Abul Fazel,* and have abridged many of its superfluities.

TALE.

"It is related that a man, mounted upon a camel, in the course of travelling arrived at a place, where others from the same caravan had lighted a fire before proceeding on their journey. The fan-like wind, breathing on the embers, had

* Abul Fazel was the vizier of the Emperor Akbar, and the translator of many Persian and Sanskreet works. The emperor, however, sensible of their defects, advised his vizier to abridge many of the tedious digressions which appeared in them.

produced a flame; and the sparks, flying over the jungle, the dry wood had become ignited, and the whole plain glowed, like a bed of tulips.

"In the midst of this was an enormous snake, who, encircled by the flames, possessed no means of escape, and was about to be broiled like a fish, or kabobed like a partridge for the table. Blood oozed from his poison-charged eyes; and, seeing the man and the camel, he thus supplicated for assistance.

COUPLET.

'What if in kindness thou vouchsafe me thy pity;
Loosen the knot with which my affairs are entangled.'

"Now the traveller was a good man, and one who feared God. When he heard the complaint of the snake, and saw his pitiable condition, he reasoned thus with himself: 'This snake is, indeed, the enemy of man, but being in trouble and perplexity, it would be most commendable in me to drop the seed of compassion; the fruit of which is prosperity in this world, and exaltation in the next.' Thus convinced, he fastened one of his saddle bags to the end of his spear, and extended it to the snake, who, delighted at escape, entered the bag, and was rescued from the flames. The man then opening the mouth of the bag, addressed him thus, 'Depart whither thou wilt, but forget not to offer up thanksgiving for thy preservation; henceforth seek the corner of retirement, and cease to afflict mankind, for they who do so are dishonest in this world and the next.'

COUPLET.

'Fear God — distress no one;
This indeed is true salvation.'

"The snake replied, 'Oh! young man, hold thy peace, for truly I will not depart, until I have wounded both thee and this camel.' The man cried out, 'But how is this? Have I not rendered thee a benefit? Why then is such to be my recompense?'

COUPLET.

'On my part there was faithfulness,
Why then this injustice upon thine?'

"The snake said, 'True, thou hast shewn mercy, but it was to an unworthy object: thou knewest me to be an agent of injury to mankind; consequently, when thou savedst me from destruction, thou subjectedst thyself to the same rule that applies to the punishment due for an evil act, committed against a worthy object.

"'Again, between the snake and man, there is a long standing enmity, and they who employ foresight, hold it as a maxim of wisdom, to bruise the head of an enemy; to thy security my destruction was necessary, but, in showing mercy, thou hast forfeited vigilance. It is now necessary that I should wound thee, that others may learn by thy example.' The man cried, 'Oh! snake, call but in the counsel of justice; in what creed is it written, or what practice declares, that evil should be returned for good, or that the pleasure of conferring benefits should be returned by injury and affliction?' The snake replied, 'Such is the practice amongst men: I act according to thy own decree: the same commodity of retribution I have purchased from thee, I also sell.'

HEMISTICH.

'Buy for one moment, that which thou sell'st for years.'

"In vain did the traveller entreat; the snake ever replying, 'I do but treat thee after the manner of men.' This the man denied: 'But, said he, 'let us call witnesses: if thou prove thy assertion, I will yield to thy will.' The snake looked round; a cow was grazing at a distance; and he said, 'Come, we will ask this cow the rights of the question.' When they came up to the cow, the snake, opening his mouth, said, 'Oh, cow, what is the recompense for benefits received?'

The cow said, 'If thou ask me after the manner of men, the return of good is always evil. For instance, I was for a long time in the service of a farmer; yearly I brought forth a calf, I supplied his house with milk and ghee; his sustenance, and the life of his children depended upon me. When I became old, and no longer produced young, he ceased to shelter me, and thrust me forth to die in the jungle. After finding forage, and roaming at my ease, I grew fat, and my old master, seeing my plump condition, yesterday brought with him a butcher to whom he has sold me, and to-day is appointed for my slaughter.'

"The snake said, 'Thou hast heard the cow; prepare to die quickly.' The man cried, 'It is not lawful to decide a case on the evidence of one witness, let us then call another.' The snake looked about and saw a tree, leafless and bare, flinging up its wild branches to the sky. 'Let us,' said he, 'appeal to this tree.' They proceeded together to the tree; and the snake opening his mouth, said, 'Oh, tree, what is the recompense for good?'

The tree said, 'Amongst men, the return for benefits are evil and injury. I will give you a proof of what I assert. I am a tree, who, though growing on one leg in this sad waste, was once flourishing and green, performing service to every one. When any of the human race, overcome with heat and travel, came this way, they rested beneath my shade, and slept beneath my branches; when the weight of repose abandoned their eyelids, they cast up their eyes to me, and said to each other, "Yon twig would do well for an arrow; that branch would serve for a plough; and from the trunk of this tree what beautiful planks might be made!" If they had an axe, or a saw, they selected my branches, and carried them away. Thus, they to whom I gave ease and rest rewarded me only with pain and affliction.'

COUPLET.

'Whilst my care overshadows him in perplexity,
He meditates only how best to root me up.'

"'Well,' said the snake, 'here are two witnesses; therefore, form thy resolution, for I must wound thee.' The man said, 'True; but the love of life is powerful, and while strength remains, it is difficult to root the love of it from the heart. Call but one more witness, and then I pledge myself to submit to his decree.' Now it so wonderfully happened, that a fox, who had been standing by, had heard all the argument, and now came forward. The snake seeing him, exclaimed, 'Behold this fox, let us ask him.' But before the man could speak, the fox cried out, 'Dost thou not know that the recompense for good is always evil? But what good hast thou done in behalf of this snake, to render thee worthy of punishment?' The man related his story. The fox replied, 'Thou seemest an intelligent person, why then dost thou tell me an untruth?'

COUPLET.

'How can it be proper for him that is wise to speak falsely?
How can it become an intelligent man to state an untruth?'

"The snake said, 'The man speaks truly, for behold the bag in which he rescued me.' The fox, putting on the garb of astonishment, said, 'How can I believe this thing? how could a large snake like thee be contained in so small a space?' The snake said, 'If thou doubt me, I will again enter the bag to prove it.' The fox said, 'Truly if I saw thee there, I could believe it, and would afterwards settle the dispute between thee and this man.' On this, the traveller again opened the bag, and the snake, annoyed at the disbelief of the fox, entered it; which observing, the fox cried out,—'Oh, young man, when thou hast caught thine enemy, shew him no quarter.'

COUPLET.

'When an enemy is vanquished, and in thy power,
It is the maxim of the wise, to show him no mercy.'

"The traveller took the hint of the fox, fastened the mouth of the bag, and, dashing it against a stone, destroyed the snake; and thus saved mankind from the evil effects of his wicked propensities.

HEMISTICH.

"To inflict death on an injurer of mankind is praiseworthy."

The fables of the Persians are the only part of their literature from which instruction can be derived. Their poetical works can in no way tend to improvement, as they contain nothing but glowing descriptions of the value of sensual enjoyments. It is, however, a subject for congratulation, that they are at least free from any histories contained in a degrading mythology, which can tend only, as it has done in India, to foster the vices and passions of men.

Few, even amongst the Brahmins, are now well versed in Sanskreet literature; but many of its didactic works, which are curious and valuable, have been translated into the Persian language, where their origin is half forgotten. Dramatic writing, however, for which the Hindu authors were so celebrated, is unknown to the Persians, as the Moslems of every country are unacquainted with the fascination and uses of theatrical exhibitions.

The professed story-tellers of Hindustan are, many of them, acquainted with the best fables of Persian writers; but although the odes of Hafiz are constantly chaunted by Natch girls and others, as a part of their professional display, the meaning of them they are seldom acquainted with.

The most remarkable circumstance characteristic of the Cutch Bhats is, that they implicitly believe the truth of every tale they relate. Their hearers are equally credulous; and thus the most marvellous fictions are told and believed as facts in the lives of veritable individuals. No good catholic ever spoke more confidently of a saintly relic, than the people of Cutch do of a sacred tree, a marvellous metamorphosis, or a deified stone; and the wildest darings of scepticism could never induce a Cutchee to doubt the actual preservation of the virtuous Soosie, or the origin of the wealth of king Lakeh.

In a country where conversation is restrained within narrow limits, where neither literature, politics, agriculture, nor social interests present subjects for discussion, and where a tropical sun matures the fancy, but enervates the bodily frame, the relation of Bhats must form a most delightful resource to the people; and I have for a moment often felt inclined to envy the undisturbed tranquillity of a long-bearded Rajpoot, as he reclined on his cushions, smoking a hookah, and listening to a little knot of Dadies, or story-tellers.

CHAPTER XIX.

ON THE ART OF DESIGN, AND THE GENERAL WANT OF INSTRUCTION IN CUTCH.

Origin of Poetry and the Fine Arts, in Cutch.—Paintings in the British Residency of Anjar.—Battle between Rama and Rawan, the King of Ceylon.—*Fac simile* of an Allegorical Painting, representing the Amicable Meeting of two Rajahs.—Patronage of the Arts by the Reigning Prince.—Persian Library at Cutch.—Original Letter from Manockjee Cursetjee, a Native of Bombay, honoured with the *soubriquet* of "the Byron of the East," to Colonel H. Pottinger, respecting the Formation of a "Native Literary Society."—A circular from the same gentleman, published in "The Oriental Christian Spectator."—Orlebar's English Scientific Lectures, in Bombay. —Enterprise and Talent of the Parsees.—Elphinstone College.—Proposed Education of Asiatic Women.

CUTCH, from its geographical position, is seldom resorted to as a thoroughfare for foreigners. This circumstance tends materially to check the progress of improvement. By mere accident, its inhabitants are acquainted with the arts of poetry, minstrelsy, and design; and as we consider the inefficient means by which they have been acquired, it is the more remarkable that so much knowledge should exist.

The Bardic art appears to have been introduced to Cutch from the neighbouring country of Sindh; and the Bhats trace their origin to the men of Summa, who are said to have migrated into this province about nine hundred years since, and are regarded as having been the progenitors of the original caste of Jharrejah chiefs.

Minstrelsy is practised all over Hindustan, where it was originally cultivated by the Brahmins; but the art of design is more rare, and seems to have been totally unknown in Cutch, until the return of Ram Sing, from Holland, when he is said to have instructed his countrymen. Yet I have been assured by many intelligent persons, who are well acquainted with Western India, that the people of Cutch far exceed the natives of other provinces in their knowledge of this art.

When we reflect, that an art hitherto practised only by civilized artists was readily acquired by a barbarous people from the instructions of one man, and that they have themselves adapted it to a variety of ornamental purposes, the very history of its acquirement by this people is a powerful evidence in favour of their natural capacity. No doubt can exist of their capability for the practice of other arts, the execution of which may depend on accuracy of eye and delicacy of touch.

FAC-SIMILE OF AN ALLEGORICAL PAINTING.

Representing the amicable meeting of the two Rajahs in the Hall of the British Residency at Anjor.

The only attempt at painting that I have seen, is in the lower room of the Residency at Anjar; but the artist has shewn himself to have been totally ignorant of either perspective or *chiar-oscuro*. The outlines, however, are good; the colours are well contrasted; and many of the groups are spirited and characteristic.

At first view, the lower end of the room seems a study from Landseer's *Monkeyana;* but, on nearer approach, it proves to be an historical painting, intended to represent the battle between Rama and Rawan, the king of Sanca, or Ceylon. Rawan is seated in his chariot, followed by his general, Hanumat, the prince of Satyrs, and surrounded by legions of monkey warriors.* Far above, in the sky, forts are demolished and burning, giant warriors are every where transfixed by arrows, each mighty as a weaver's beam, and the whole is as fearful a scene of bloodshed and confusion, as red, green, and yellow paint could make it.

The wall at the upper end of the room is embellished by a painting, of which the accompanying is a *fac simile,* and as such may afford a good specimen of the whole. It is intended to represent the amicable meeting of two Rajahs, one of

* The giant Rawan is said to have been commander-in-chief of a numerous and intrepid race of monkeys, by some writers denominated Indian Satyrs.

whom is attended by an Upsura, or nymph of Paradise. Ganesa, the god of wisdom, presides over the conference, and is attended by his favourite rats; below him kneels Varuna, the genius of rivers, from whose head flows the Ganges and the Jumna. The peacock appears, as sacred to Parvati, the Indian Juno; but I do not discern either the mystery of the archer, or of the animals he is pursuing, as they are not of the kinds sacred to the Hindu gods.

The sides of the room are decorated with representations of tigers, fighting elephants, and bands of gaily equipped horsemen, all characteristic, and well drawn.

The Rao is particularly anxious that his people should improve in the art of drawing; and I think they might soon acquire the requisite degree of cultivation. The practice of the art must of course be confined to Hindu artists, as the tenets of the Koran strictly forbid any representation of the Creator's works. The Mahomedans have a more exuberant fancy than the Hindus, and are better calculated for poets; but the Hindus have greater delicacy of touch, greater accuracy in imitation, and are very superior to them in perseverance. Not deficient in apprehension, they seem most adapted to receive instruction.

The Rao, who has enjoyed the advantage of

an early English education—first under the tuition of the Rev. Mr. Grey,* and subsequently, until called to the throne, under the care of Lieut. Crofton, of Her Majesty's Service, —appreciates the value of learning, and is desirous that his people should become enlightened. There is no information, however, to be acquired in Bhooj, and the people must become wiser, ere they seek it elsewhere. An old Mahomedan Synd possesses a very good library in the town, containing some valuable Persian books; but neither the white-bearded bibliothecary himself, nor any of his visitors, can solve the mysteries of a single character.†

Manockjee Cursetjee, Esq. a well educated

* Mr. Grey is well known to the world as the friend of the poet Burns, who freqnently alludes to him in his correspondence. Mr. Grey was buried in the grave-yard at Bhooj, and his Highness the Rao has long been desirous of erecting a monument to the memory of his amiable and lamented tutor.

† The Musjid, in which this library is contained, is the property of a Synd, whose father was invited from Delhi to Bhooj by Rao Rahiden, when that prince became a Mahomedan. It is enclosed, and has fine terraces, with a reservoir sixty feet deep. The library contains about one thousand Persian and Arabic manuscripts, principally treating of religious and historical subjects. The Synd, a very fat and foolish descendant of the Prophet, guards them with a most jealous eye, being firmly convinced that some of them are works on chemistry, and contain a true recipe for the philosopher's stone!

native gentleman in Bombay, better known, perhaps, by his *sobriquet* of the "Byron of the East," addressed a letter, some time since, to the Rao, requesting him to become the patron of a native literary society; but the Rao, with his characteristic modesty, declined. The following note, addressed to the British resident on the subject, may be considered curious.

"To Col. H. Pottinger,
&c., &c., &c. 27, *July*, 1836. *Bombay.*

"MY DEAR SIR,

"I have not as yet been honoured with a reply from his Highness of Cutch, to the letter I gave you some time ago, nor have the good fortune of hearing from you on the subject. Owing, however, to the excess of doing among our *Shetts** in this commercial season of the year, nothing has yet been done with respect to the formation of the "Native Literary Society;" but as all the China-men (with the exception of one or two) have now cleared this port, I hope soon to be able to resume the subject with my distinguished friends. In the mean time, if through your kind offices I could get a few lines from the Rao, in acknowledging the receipt of my said letter, and assuring that his Highness will support the institution when formed, it will be a great help to me,

* A native term for our Esquires.

as it will be a great stimulus to the Gent. here. I entreat you, therefore, to put a few words to his Highness, and let me soon hear the result. I have written our esteemed friend, Captain Burnes, rather fully upon the subject by this opportunity.

"Believe me,
"Colonel,
"Ever yours with respect,
"Most faithfully,
"MANOCKJEE CURSETJEE."

The following circular letter, published by the same gentleman in the *Oriental Christian Spectator*, is also interesting, as it evinces the capacity the Hindu intellect possesses for the appreciation of the exact sciences; and it is illustrative of the probable advantages which might be derived from a series of public lectures on subjects calculated to excite the interest of a native population.

"MY DEAR FRIENDS,

"As you seem all anxious to make a respectable progress in acquiring English literature, as your sincere friend, I would humbly advise you to give up, once a week, your carriage, horses, and evening drive, and attend Mr. Orlebar's public lecture at the Town Hall, which is to be delivered every Friday evening at five o'clock. Though no public notification is made or circular sent round, in the shape of an invitation, it is, as says last week's *Darpan*,* 'open to all without distinction.'

"The primary discourse of the lectures delivered last Friday, as abstracted, as you will see in this day's *Darpan*, so well explains the utility of the mathematical science, and prepares one to enjoy the exquisite pleasure to be derived from it, that I would not waste words with a recapitulation to induce your going to the lecture room. All I can say is, read (if you have not read) this day's *Darpan*, and fix your mind to what this proverb says, 'Emulation seldom fails to reward.'

"You would not be offended, I am sure, with this my humble address, if I may call it so, and with the frankness of its expression, when I assure you that I do so, with no other feeling than that of fraternity — being

"Yours, sincere and attached,

"MANOCKJEE CURSETJEE."

We have long known the Parsees in Bombay to be an enterprising and energetic race of men, capable of acquiring every description of commercial information; but here is one amongst them talking with enthusiasm of the mathematics,

* A remarkably well conducted native paper, published weekly in Bombay.

and liberally urging his native friends to participate in his intellectual enjoyments. Such is the effect of culture, and such might be equally its effects on any native society, were similar means to be adopted. I have but lately received the assurance from my most amiable and intelligent friend, Synd Azamoo Deen Hassan,* that he considers the intellect of the Cutchees peculiarly adapted for the study of mathematics. I sincerely trust that the good seed sown by the able professors of the Elphinstone College may take root, and spread; and although I scarcely hope to see a Laplace amongst the inhabitants of Bhooj, experience certainly affords us reason to believe, that no mental incapability exists, which should tend to oppose any system for progressive improvement, if advanced by rational and considerate means, founded on a knowledge of the native character, and adapted for the introduction of the useful arts. The women of Cutch, both Mahomedan and Hindu, display much greater quickness of apprehension than their lords; and as it is the custom in the East to allow lads to remain in the Harem until they attain the

* The Śynd was lately in the service of Lord William Bentinck, as a Moonshee. He is now the British agent at the mouth of the Indus. He is equally amiable and intelligent, and as a student was considered the flower of the Calcutta College.

age of fourteen, unusual advantages would arise in India from educating the native women, whose influence might then produce impressions on the minds of their sons highly advantageous to their future improvement. I do not think the inclination would be found wanting to profit by such opportunities if they could be provided. As an instance of the contrary, a highly respectable Mahomedan in Bhooj, who has no fewer than seven daughters, lately expressed a wish to find some respectable European women, who would undertake to educate them in the English language. The prejudices of the natives, however, present great obstacles to the success of such an attempt; as any European who consents to become their instructress, must herself become almost a prisoner in the Harem; and it would be long ere the native women could be sufficiently educated to become the teachers of their countrywomen.

Yet there is not one opposing prejudice, in the history of progress, which wisdom, energy, and perseverance will not overcome; and therefore, I hold the future emancipation and civilized condition of Asiatic women, as one of the great articles of my social faith.

CHAPTER XX.

JUGGLING, SNAKE-CHARMING, AND MAGIC.

Professions of the Kalatnee Caste.—Jugglers.—Exhibition, and Musical Instrument, of a Snake-charmer.—Tricks and Impostures.—Sacredness of the Cobra Capella.—Sanc'ha-Nágà, the King of the Snakes.—A Snake Legend.—Magical Arts.—Trial by Ordeal.—Practice of "Traga."—Singular Mode of recovering Debts.

THE Kalatnee caste, in Cutch, adopt a great variety of professions: some adapted only for amusement, and others calculated to attract attention from the respect in which mysterious arts are held by an ignorant and superstitious people. Some of this caste are mere tumblers, others practise jugglery in all its branches; some profess to be capable of charming the most venomous snakes, and others earn a livelihood as magicians, without the trouble of displaying any mechanical expertness; and they are perhaps the most successful. The jugglers practise the tricks common to their class all over India: they thread beads with the tongue, play with clasp knives, balance poles, with wonderful precision; and conclude by swallowing a Damascus blade, as their favourite and most telling feat.

The Sampuris, or snake charmers, are a caste well known in India; and though perhaps not entirely deserving the title of impostors, they are undoubtedly a shrewd, cunning, and abundantly fraudulent race, who almost equal the Brahmins in the art of imposing on the credulity of the people. That the beautiful description of snake, known as the Cobra Capella, may be attracted by a peculiar sound is possible, and undoubtedly they are at times so seduced from their hiding-places, and captured by the Sampuri. Generally, however, a succession of tricks are amusingly displayed by the artist, who ingeniously contrives to introduce one of his own snakes already trained for his purpose. A Sampuri always makes an agreement with his employer that the snake shall not be killed; and thus one cunningly brought in his cummerbund, first dropped, and then at a fitting opportunity again caught near a suspected place, is quite sufficient to excite the wonder and awe of the spectators, and procure for the artist, the rupee, or half a rupee, promised to his success.

A short time since, a Sampuri made his salaam to us, intending to display his skill, and from him I learnt the secrets of his calling. The man was shrewd, good humoured, and active: he wore a red turban decorated with two bunches of pink feathers; under one arm he carried a small bundle, and from the other was suspended the instrument whose sound is supposed capable of charming the most venomous snakes. In form it resembled a double flageolet passed through the centre of a small gourd; but its sound far exceeded in harshness anything I have ever heard, except perhaps the bagpipe, whose drone it was somewhat like.

On the Sampuri's uncovering a small basket, a large and beautiful cobra raised itself perpendicularly, with the undulating motion peculiar to its species; and, spreading its hood, the apparently enraged reptile commenced a series of attacks upon its keeper, who, seizing it by the throat, affected to coax and play with it caressingly. He afterwards stated that it would readily take milk, or any description of appropriate sustenance ; but, when the milk was brought, the Sampuri seemed to regret having given it such a character for docility as a messmate, and was constrained to administer the liquid by means of an ivory funnel, which, with an iron stile, he forced into the reptile's throat.

The venom had been removed, but the fangs still remained ; and the Sampuri, in describing his manner of removing the poison, made no allusion to the "precious jewel," or celebrated snake stone, mentioned by Major Moore.*

In a remarkably small canvas bag, the Sampuri carried a second snake : it was large, and of a bright orange colour, relieved by black spots. This sort of snake is common in Cutch, and is called by the natives, the Lohar, or worker of iron. The Sampuri, I have no doubt, intended that this snake should remain perdue ; and had we consented to a display of his art, he would cunningly have watched his opportunity, and then,

* Major Moore states, that the species of snake called Cobra Capella, exclusively "wears the precious jewel in its crown," which is called the snake stone ; this being taken out of the head of the reptile he is no longer venomous. *Vide* "*Oriental Fragments.*"

after a little piping on his calabash, he would have exultingly captured this poor reptile, and accused it of being the depredator of our fowl-house.

This snake, the Sampuri assured us, had been caught only a few days before; and he set it at liberty in the garden, and recaught it for our amusement. The method of actually catching the snake, in the first instance, is curious, and requires great coolness and dexterity. The snake-catcher is provided with two long bamboos: the first he at once fixes on the reptile's tail, and rapidly slipping the other horizontally along his body, he seizes him by the throat, and, holding him tightly with one hand, despite all his writhing and wriggling, extracts the venom with a small hook. This done, the captive soon discovers its defenceless state, and is readily tamed.

The natives regard the whole as the result of magic; and, as magicians, fear, respect, and support the Sampuris who practise these arts. Of course, the Sampuris exercise all the tricks of their profession, to sustain an opinion which thus conveniently ministers so much to their advantage. The people of Cutch are more credulous than the generality of Asiatics; but a circumstance which tends to increase the belief on this subject, is the opinion which the Hindus entertain generally, of the power of snakes, and of their sacred character; together with the effect produced on their imaginations, by numerous legends connected with their nature and history. Even were a Cobra Capella to cause the death of half a village, a Hindu would not suffer it to be killed, lest he should bring on himself and family the wrath of Sanc'ha-Nágà, the king of the snakes.* It is not remarkable, therefore, that a mortal who can once conquer a being so powerful should, in their opinion, be either a friend and equal of Naga, or by the power of magic be rendered superior to him.

* The king of serpents, according to the Hindu books, formerly reigned on a mountain called Chacragiri, very much to the eastward; but by the power of his rival Garudá (an immense vulture) his subjects were compelled to supply that enormous bird with a snake every day. The king, however, declined to give up his serpentine subjects; and the enraged Garudá compelled him to take refuge with a superior deity.

The breath of Sanc'ha Nágà is believed by the Hindus to be a fiery, poisonous wind; and, by this legend, they account for the dreadful effects of the Samoom, a hot envenomed wind, which is said to blow from the mountains of Hubáb, where the serpent resides, through the whole of the desert.

Two holy men, Rishis, undertook to render this royal snake tractable, and even reduced his size so much, as to carry him about in an earthen pot; and crowds of people are now said to worship him at the place of his residence, near the river Cali.

"They," (says the Indian writer) "who perform yearly and daily rites in honour of Sanc'ha Nágà, will acquire immense riches."—*Asiatic Researches*, vol. iii.

The native idea of the employment of magic is not confined to snake-charming; but whatever unusual circumstance may happen is at once supposed to owe its origin to some practice of the occult sciences. An instance of this occurred a short time since between two rival goldsmiths, in which one of them publicly accused the other, at the Rao's Durbar, of having employed the arts of magic, to oppress and ruin him. From the same state of ignorance which fosters this favourite superstition has arisen the mischievous system of a trial by ordeal. In Cutch, this is frequently resorted to in cases of theft, and is of various forms; all, however, tending to certify the guilt of the suspected person, in the same spirit by which the charge of witchcraft was established amongst us in olden times. Thus, in one favourite mode of trial, the accused is condemned to plunge headlong into a river; and, if he come out dry, he is considered innocent. Another form condemns him to dip his hands into boiling oil, on the same terms. There are many other forms, all holding forth little chance of escape to the victim; yet so satisfied are the poor people of the justice of this mode of proceeding, that a suspected person never attempts to evade the trial. If innocent, he discovers his error too late; for every one around, who witnesses his sufferings, becomes at once satisfied of his guilt, and sees no reason to question the fairness of the means by which it has been proved. In Sindh, the trial by ordeal is even more common than it is in Cutch.

The system of "Traga," as another branch of superstitious faith, I have already mentioned. It is firmly believed, that any person choosing to commit Traga can, by this means, bring down a severe and perpetual curse upon its object; one that shall slay his family, wither his crops, and destroy all that he has. A modification of Traga is frequently adopted for the purpose of recovering small debts; and some idea of the awe inspired by the custom may be gained from the fact, that the Charons, who most practise it, are, as grain merchants, exempted from many of the import duties, paying only about one-half the sum levied on others.* They have also a similar

* The caste of "Charons," of whom previous mention has been made, are by profession grain-merchants, who travel over large tracts of country, and possess herds of three or four hundred bullocks, which accompany them on their tedious marches. As a caste, they are both feared and respected. As a proof of the latter, they smoke the same hookah with the Rajpoots; this custom being considered as an unquestionable allowance of equality between different castes in India. During the most unsettled times in Cutch, when it was unsafe for the merchant to travel even from village to village without an escort, and the cultivator sold his grain with his sword by his side, the Charon was always exempted from even a chance of molestation.

custom, called "Dhurna," according to which a creditor may seat himself at a debtor's door, and refuse to eat, drink, or sleep until the debt is paid. If he die in this state, his debtor is supposed to be held answerable to the gods; and such is the dread of this extensive system of dunning, that a man who becomes "Dhurna," is sure to succeed in his object.

Such, amongst a barbarous people, are sometimes the only means of enforcing or obtaining justice; and superstitious fears become too frequently the only protection for life and property.

CHAPTER XXI.

PRODUCTIONS OF CUTCH.

Nature of the Soil.—Native Ignorance of Agriculture.—Grain.—Fruits.—Plants. —English Vegetables.—Irrigation.—The Kheie. — Milk-bush.—Sindhian Cotton Tree.—Superior Fruits.—Climate.—Flowering Shrubs. —Locusts.—Sheep.—Goats.—Buffaloes —Horses.—Bullocks.—Asses.—Dogs. — Camels.—Modes of Camel-riding.—Wild Animals.—Alum Mines.—Method of purifying Alum.—Coal Veins.—Fossil Remains.—Basalt.—Saltpetre.—Natural History.—Physical, Moral, Religious, and Intellectual state of the Inhabitants of Cutch.—Ancient History of the Country.—Commerce.—Education.—Colleges of Bombay and Calcutta.—Climate and Temperature of Cutch.—Thermometrical Summary for the Spring and Summer Months of the Year 1837.

THE soil of Cutch is sandy, and agriculture is so little understood, and conducted in so slovenly a manner, that the produce of the scattered plantations is small, and the province does not produce half that is required for its own consumption. The usual native grains* are cultivated; and in

* The *Holcus Spicatus*, or Bajiree; the *Holcus Saccharatus*, or Jewarree; the *Phaseolus Mungo*, or Moong; the *Dolichas Fabœformis*, or Gowar; and the *Phaseolus Aconitifolius*, or Mut.

the eastern parts of the province, wheat, barley, and sugar-cane. The principal trees growing without culture, are the Baubool,* the Peepul,† the Bair,‡ the Date, and the common Neem.|| The Bokhara Neem is cultivated, and bears a peculiarly delicate and sweet-scented blossom, resembling, at a short distance, the Persian lilac. The Castor plant§ is common all over the province; and its broad glossy leaves, and fine clusters of crimson berries, are very ornamental. In gardens attached to the bungalows in the camp of Bhooj, the growth of English vegetables has been tried with great success. Tomatas, cabbages, cauliflowers, peas, beans, potatoes, and all sorts of pot-herbs, flourish and produce good crops. The climate seems adapted to them, and they require only constant irrigation during the hot season, to preserve them in luxuriance. This is easily effected: each garden is provided with a well, from which the water is conducted, by channels, all over the plots which require irrigation. The water is drawn up from the wells in leathern bags, by a pair of sturdy bullocks, yoked to ropes in length about the depth of the well: the bullocks are driven down an inclined plane, which brings the bag to the surface, and causes the water to fall over into a reservoir, whence it

* *Mimosa Arabica.* † *Ficus Religiosa.* ‡ *Jujube.*
|| *Melia Azadarachta.* § *Palma Christi.*

runs into the different channels, and irrigates the whole of the garden in two or three hours. As the bag empties itself, the bullocks are scientifically backed to the brink of the well, when the bag descends, refills, and is brought again to the surface; the ropes running over a large, well oiled, wooden roller. The driver sits on the ropes; and, as the bullocks draw up the bag, he cheers them on with cries, or urges them by the more impressive argument of tail-twisting, the motive of which is well understood in its application.

Cutch, although its general appearance is arid and sandy in the extreme, is diversified in the neighbourhood of its towns and villages by patches of cultivation; and where these fail, the soil is nearly covered with a stunted thorny sort of brushwood, and a singular kind of bramble, called the Kheie. This plant grows to a height of about five feet, and has a smooth green stem perfectly leafless: it bears clusters of bright red blossoms, which the natives pickle, and also use in their *Materia Medica*, with the castor oil and plantain-leaf. The plantations and gardens are surrounded by hedges of the milk bush,* the juice of which is particularly pungent, and blisters the skin if touched by it. The men employed to cut these hedges have their faces protected by a sail-cloth mask. I have mentioned the prickly pear

* A species of euphorbia, called by the natives "Tour."

already: it grows over every part of Cutch, and gives a welcome appearance of vegetation to the black and rocky hills, although known to be peculiarly the growth of the most sterile soils.

The Sindhian cotton flourishes here, and is deserving notice. The tree grows to the height of about six feet, and has glossy and beautifully veined leaves: those which conceal the pod are arranged in a triangle, surmounted by a delicate straw-coloured blossom, that falls off as the cotton ripens and swells in the pod, the pod itself resembling an acorn, and growing in the centre of the little triangle of leaves.

The Sindhians affirm, that with them this fine plant grows to such an enormous size, that men are compelled to gather the cotton on horseback; and that, like the golden fruit of the Hesperides, its produce is guarded by huge monsters, servants of Naga, the prince of snakes. These they are compelled to destroy, before they can secure the prize.* The common native fruits do not attain perfection in Cutch: the mangoes, guavas, plantains, shaddocks, and pomegranates, are all of an inferior kind. The best fruits produced are, the common white grape; the small sweet black grape, or kismus, of Persia; and the musk

* The common cotton-plant grows abundantly all over the Kantar, or coast of Cutch, but is too well known to require particular notice.

melons, which grow in vast luxuriance in the dry beds of rivers: the roots, striking downwards, soon meet the desired moisture; and the fruit and leaves, resting on the dry sand, under the influence of a tropical sun, ripen speedily into a good size and fine flavour. Cutch possesses, in its peculiar climate, considerable advantages for both animal and vegetable life. During the hottest season, the evenings and nights are uniformly cool; and even when the thermometer rises to 130° in the mid-day sun, immediately on its setting, a cool breeze springs up from the westward, and refreshes every thing that has life.

The rains are usually slight, and the climate must be considered healthy; although, at the close of the rainy season, cases of fever are prevalent, and during the cold season, rheumatism. Liver complaints are not common; and although disease, in various forms, abounds amongst the native population, it may, I believe, be more readily traced to the dissipated habits of the people, than to a general insalubrity of climate.

The water of Bhooj is hard and unwholesome: the natives of other provinces are greatly prejudiced against it. The common saying, however, "that should a saint drink the water of Bhooj he would prove treacherous,"* is rather to be con-

* See Captain McMurdo's able paper in the *Bombay Society's Literary Transactions.*

sidered as expressive of their opinion of the moral evil of the city and its inhabitants, than of its limpid streams.

The brilliant and sweetly scented oleander grows without culture, and hedges of it may be seen near Anjar. It is increased by layers ; and the single and double, the white, crimson, and delicate rose-coloured species, all grow rapidly.

The sweet and wax-like Mogree is common : it is well known as the favourite flower which the Hindu females use, to wreath into garlands, both for their personal decoration and for the temples of their gods. They mix with it the bright yellow blossom of the *Verbesina Sativa*, a field produce, but gay and showy in its appearance, resembling the Chumpa,* but less fragrant.

A great scarcity of grain has frequently produced the evil effects of famine in Cutch when the rains have fallen slightly for several consecutive seasons ; and the evil of this want of sufficient produce has been aggravated, by the sudden appearance of flocks of locusts, which literally screened us from the light of day, and devoured every green thing, until a keen north wind carried them into the sea. I have seen these destructive insects clinging so closely together on the Neem trees in our garden, that the slight branches were bowed by them ; and when, on

* A tree sacred to the Hindus.

shaking the stem, they flew off for a moment, the tree was enveloped by them, like a cloud. The natives eat them as curry, and esteem them delicate food.* I have heard their flavour described as nearly resembling that of prawns. The Arabs eat them both dried and fresh.

The pasture in the gorges of the hills is good, and the Cutch sheep are esteemed excellent; their wool is peculiarly dark-coloured, and their heads are awkwardly shaped. The goats are a large grave looking race; and, with their black bodies and long white pendent ears, remind one of my lord chancellor, in gown and wig. These useful animals are prized, in their due proportion, with the black buffaloe, each affording a principal source of sustenance to the natives. Nothing can be more uncouth than the figures of the huge buffaloes, with their long heads, curved horns, and a black bald-looking hide, generally encrusted with dried mud. Few artificial arrangements, however, can produce the idea of luxurious refreshment so fully, as may be gained by standing on the bank of one of the numerous tanks with which Indian cities abound, and at a bright sunset, while the shadows of the tall palm-trees are lengthening, when the sun is still lingering above

* Herodotus mentions, that the Nasamones were accustomed to hunt for locusts, which, having dried in the sun, they reduced to a powder, and ate, mixed with milk. Book iv.

the horizon, and the earth is uncooled by the evening breeze, to watch the herds of buffaloes return half suffocated and weary to the city, plunging as they do into the cool waters, and swimming eagerly forward, until, having gained the middle of the tank, they pause to abandon themselves to the luxury of the time, flinging the water over their huge frames, and indulging in all sorts of mirthful contortions.

Horses are never used in husbandry, the required labour being performed by bullocks, which, with camels, are also employed for carrying heavy baggage, grain, and merchandise. The horses are trained to an easy and peculiar ambling pace, and are fleet only for short distances. The common native love of corpulence extends even to the treatment of their steeds, by rich men, who, to produce this desired effect, feed them to repletion with grain, ghee, and sugar.

The ponies, or tattus, as they are called in India, are a miserable race, used only for baggage, or the conveyance of some antique member of a family, under whose weight, increased by, perhaps, a child, a pair of well stuffed saddle-bags, and a hookah, they trudge along with an endurance of fatigue truly admirable.

Asses are used by grain merchants, and potters, but they are a small, untractable, and abundantly noisy race. When dismissed from labour, they are not considered worth their provender, and are, therefore, left to roam about the plains, joining their most unmusical but sonorous plaints with those of the Pariah dogs, by which they add few charms to the constrained vigils of a traveller in the East.*

* It is customary, in travelling, to pitch tents in a plain near some village for the convenience of supplies; but the combined annoyances of dogs, who are a most watchful race — of asses, who scour in herds over the plains—and of wandering bullocks, who are incessantly entangling themselves in the tent ropes — allow shelter indeed, but little rest.

Camels are much used in Cutch: they are brought principally from Marwar and Sindh, where they are bred in great abundance. Young, slight, and well-bred camels are trained for the saddle, and become extremely fleet, travelling at the rate of about eight miles an hour. In some parts of Cutch, herds of camels are to be seen browsing together on the stunted shrubs of the jungle. These are the property of Mahomedan priests, or peers, who hold them sacred, and exempt them from all labour for the sake of the Prophet, "on whom be peace!" Many of these camels are decorated with collars of white beads, and are handsome, and well bred. The camel has always been used for riding in Cutch, and its utility in a country so remarkable for its sandy and sterile nature is incalculable. The paces of these animals, when well trained, are far from uneasy; the difficulty of mounting is perhaps most objectionable to the rider. Captain Mc Murdo's account of the manner of driving the camel, in Sindh, so perfectly agrees with that which is common in Cutch, that I use his words, as peculiarly descriptive. "In Sindh, where people of the first rank do not consider it beneath their dignity to ride on the camel, so much attention is paid to the comfort, and, indeed, elegance of the saddle, that the motion is rendered more tolerable than it is in other countries where the animal is in less repute. On the saddles, which are often made of embroidered broad cloth, are two seats, the foremost of which is occupied by the person who manages the camel, which he effects by means of a string attached to a piece of wood about two inches in length, with a knob at each end, passed through a perforation in the nostril; the seat in the rear is filled by an armed person, who acts as an attendant and guard."

Some other uses to which camels are applied are still unnoticed. They are constantly seen attached to mills for expressing oil,* and the milk of the female is drunk, and considered particularly wholesome.

The other animals abounding in Cutch, are the niel-ghye, deer, antelope, cheetah, or hunting leopard, hyena, wild cat, &c. The desert rat, a species of jerboa, is common; and this mischievous little miner makes innumerable holes over the whole surface of the sandy plains, which, from their size, are highly inconvenient, and even dangerous to horsemen. The destructive powers of an animal of a similar description are mentioned by Mr. Elphinstone, in his interesting "Account of the Kingdom of Caubul."

* It may be remarked here, as at Constantinople, that the men engaged in expressing oil, and the oil porters, are amongst the stoutest and sturdiest men of the country.

ALUM MINES.

On the north and east sides of the village of Mhurr are some very productive alum mines, which were discovered by a Mahomedan Jogie, from Sindh. They now form a monopoly in right of the Rao of Cutch. These mines are constantly worked, and the system of refining the alum by a process of burning and boiling seems perfectly understood by the miners, who work during the dry season, in five pits lighted by small oil lamps. The roof of these pits is so formed, and secured by arches, that little danger can be dreaded of its falling in, or injuring the workmen. Each mine is about thirty feet deep, and forty wide, excavated horizontally. About four hundred men are constantly employed in the mines, and sixty thousand Cutch maunds* of alum have been produced from them in one year.

The process of refining the alum is curious: after being taken from the mine it is first burnt, and, from the appearance of clay, assumes that of grey sulphur, and is called Tooree. It is then thrown into the bed of a river, secured by banks of earth; when the alum, by the water passing over it, acquires a greenish hue, and becomes porous. Boiled with an alkali, called Soraka,†

* A maund is equal to about twenty-five English pounds.

† Muriate of ammonia.

for about two hours, it is then poured into jars, and for the first time assumes the proper appearance of alum. Its purification, however, is considered incomplete, until it has been again boiled. It is then poured into earthen vessels, and buried in the ground: after a short time, the vessels are broken, and the alum, which retains the form of the chatty, is packed on asses or bullocks, and sent to the coast for exportation.

These are the only mines at present worked in Cutch. Veins of coal have been found in several parts of the Eastern side of the province; but the expense of boring has not been repaid by a sufficient quantity of coal; and the work has in consequence been discontinued. It appears from the *strata* passed through in boring, that a great resemblance exists between the character of the sections here and in the coal counties in England; and this allows the inference, that coal might be found in considerable quantities, could the boring be continued under able superintendence. Perhaps, as the Steam Navigation of the river Indus shall become important to our commercial interests, the Bombay government may consider it worth while to entrust some practical miners with the prosecution of the work.

The nullahs and hills of Cutch abound with most curious fossil remains, calculated to throw much light on the labours of the Eastern geologist.

Near the Runn, some superb specimens of ammonite have been found, encrusted with a delicate tracery of sea-weed. Many of these specimens have been forwarded to the societies of London, where they cannot fail of exciting a lively interest.

Red sand-stone also abounds; and near Anjar are some fine specimens of Columnar Basalt. Saltpetre is produced in the neighbourhood of Bhooj, and is purified in a factory close to the town. The consequent cheapness of this luxury in a tropical climate is gratefully felt; although in Cutch, as in most stations in the interior of our Indian possessions, the hot winds render its use for cooling liquids needless. During the hot season, the petticoated bottles, after being inundated with water, are placed under the influence of a scorching wind, which sweeps like a sirocco over the barren plains; and, fearful as are its other effects, it makes some amends by cooling our wine and sherbet most deliciously.

Every one who has gasped under an Indian sun, must remember, with a pleasureable sensation, the refreshment he has enjoyed by this means, and the real luxury of a cup of cold water thus preserved in its original freshness.*

* The water is cooled in earthen vessels called Coojahs. They are of very elegant forms, and extremely porous. The most curious are stated to be made from the clay of the celebrated well of Zem-zem.

During the last two years, ice has been introduced into India from America; but, being expensive, and difficult to preserve, its use will be confined to the Presidency, where it is usually seen, handed round the dinner table, in little blocks, or used for producing the guava, pomegranate, mangoe, and pine apple ices.

On noticing the productions of Cutch, it evidently appears, that a large field for observation and inquiry is open to the naturalist, of a kind unusually interesting. The extreme northerly position of this province renders it little known; and while it possesses abundant subjects for scientific investigation, its fame rests chiefly on the high character it has obtained for good sport. The natives have very little intelligence, and proportionably little curiosity; few of them have ever left their own province; and many have never been to the coast, or beyond their neighbouring village. In the case of one or two individuals, who have been, by some unusual circumstances, educated a little in advance of their countrymen, good capacity has been displayed, and an inclination for improvement. It is, therefore, to be regretted, that no means exist, by which the people might acquire a knowledge of the useful arts. During the reign of the present Rao, and the able administration of public affairs by Colonel Pottinger, the tranquillity of the country has remained undisturbed; and having ceased to experience the calamities of a civil war, the majority of the people have sunk into a state of supineness, instead of occupying themselves, during the security of peace, with the care of improving and fertilizing their province. Cutch has undoubtedly a soil unfriendly to cultivation; yet in all cases where sufficient industry has been exerted, the results have been favourable. A higher stimulus, however, is required, than at present exists. The people have few wants, and are habitually indolent; and their implements of husbandry are so rude and ill constructed, that labour is not repaid by a proportionable result. It may not be considered Utopian to hope, that, in a few years, English agriculturists may be induced to apply for grants of land, under the native princes, and introduce an improved system of farming into our Indian provinces. In common with all inferior beings, the natives of India are strongly imbued with cunning, which particularly inclines them to any matter immediately connected with their self-interest. This particular cast of mind, with its consequent acquisitiveness, seems the point to which our endeavours should tend, if we desire their general improvement; and I think, that a knowledge of the principles of agriculture might be advantageously inculcated, and might lead them to an acquaintance with the elements of the mechanical sciences, and the useful arts, adapted to the ordinary concerns of daily life. Such acquirements might eventually exert a greater influence in rendering them reflecting and rational beings, than can ever be effected by means calculated to alarm their religious prejudices, and to bring the whole strength of the Brahminical priesthood in array against us.

In the desired object of converting the Hindus to Christianity, we should, I think, end where we now begin. Our efforts at present are made by teaching the people English,* and by instructing them in the tenets of the Christian religion, which they must either disbelieve and reject, or believe and adopt. If the latter, they must become outcasts from their tribe; and thus, from falling into disrespect and contempt amongst their countrymen, lose that influence over their minds, by which alone the object of general good could be attained.

History tells us, that before the Eastern empire fell under the Ottoman dominion, it was the

* Early association attaches men to the language of their country, and renders any information conveyed through its medium far more attractive than when clothed in the signs of another tongue; and even were it otherwise, the time bestowed on acquiring a foreign language might be better employed by gaining new and useful ideas in their own.

seat of all the learning which remained in the world. The Arabs appear to have been literary, polished, and humane, and to have made great proficiency in many of the arts. Persia, also, is said to have been the vast repository for all the learning of the ancient Egyptians; and India herself, rich in oriental wealth, traded with Italy, Persia, and Egypt, and, by the enterprise of her merchants, monopolized the commerce of the Eastern world. Many noble monuments of the wealth of India yet remain, and many proofs of the acquaintance of its people with the arts of civilized life ; but now, their energies have failed, and their power is laid low ; their self-interest has lost its stimulus, and their learning is forgotten. The priesthood have secured all influence to themselves. To prevent the dangerous chance of a coalition amongst the people, they have adopted the systematic policy of dividing them into castes, and promoting a spirit of disunion, on which their power is founded.

The annals of India present, indeed, a dark page in the history of nations. Her commerce, which was once of sufficient importance and magnitude to excite in the Tyrians, Egyptians, and Venetians, a desire for traffic, is now confined to the export of a few natural productions of comparatively little value ; and the produce of her far-famed looms, once so highly coveted by the rich and the fair, is exchanged for a manufacture of coarse cloths; whilst the raw cotton which her fields produce is sent to England, to be manufactured into a fabric designed for exportation to the Indian market.

This change is natural, and its evil effects will continue so long as circumstances may oppose the desirable re-action that is required, to arouse the natives of India from their present lethargy and moral degradation.

A knowledge of agriculture, and of commerce, as its necessary result, are the two first steps which must be taken by all people emerging from barbarism into civilization. These originate a change in the condition of nations, which is perfected by progressive and general improvement, until the arts, sciences, literature, and religion of civilized life, banish the horrors attendant on a barbarous state.

It is true, that, in the presidencies of Bombay and Calcutta, colleges are endowed, which, supplied by able professors, afford to the native population great facilities for the acquirement of learning; but these advantages are circumscribed, and inefficient for the purpose of general improvement. The natives, so educated, obtain lucrative appointments, which establish them in the large stations, whilst the great mass of the people remain in the darkest ignorance. If grants of land could be cultivated by English colonists—if elementary works on agriculture, the useful arts, and the first principles of natural philosophy, were to be translated into, and published in, the native languages, and intelligent native teachers directed to explain and read them to the people — I believe much general good might be effected. The reasoning faculties of the natives once exercised, and curiosity and interest once awakened, their own intelligence would work the rest; and in this way only do I think that the barriers of caste can ever be lowered in India, the Brahminical power be abolished, or the country regain its sources of wealth and consideration.

CLIMATE AND TEMPERATURE OF CUTCH.

Having elsewhere remarked on the peculiarities of the climate of this country, I here subjoin a thermometrical summary for the spring and summer months of the year 1837, which was remarkable for heat, and for a great scarcity of rain.

The variations of temperature in this province are very unusual. The maximum and minimum points, I have myself seen, were 28° and 109°.

Both were observed in tents; the one in the month of January, and the other in June, during the year 1835. The cold during the winter is frequently intense, and ice is very commonly observed on water standing in vessels during the night, and exposed to the air.

The monsoon is usually slight. The prevailing winds are from the W. to S.W.; and the latter, contrary to the general experience of other parts of this side of India, are, in this province, preventives of rain. When these winds blow frequently during the monsoon months of July, August, and September, they are always observed to cause drought and scarcity. For this reason, the natives distinguish these winds, as the "Handie Phors," or literally, "the breakers of the pot."

The monsoon, in Cutch, may be generally expected to set in, at the end of June, or the beginning of July. It invariably blows over with the wind from the N.E. The air, during the rains, is close and oppressive; the falls of rain being preceded by violent storms of thunder and lightning.

THERMOMETRICAL SUMMARY for the following Months at the Station of Bhooj, in the Province of Cutch.

Camp, Bhooj, at Lat. N. 23° 14′ 14″; Long. 69° 45′ 0″.

MONTHS 1837.	Maximum.	Minimum.	Mean.	Average Maximum.	Average Minimum.	Average Mean.	Greatest diurnal Range.	Least diurnal Range.	Average diurnal Range.	Prevailing Winds.	REMARKS.
APRIL.	104°	76°	90°	95°	74°	84½	29°	15°	21°	W.S.W.	Thermometer. In the Sun 130°. Clear, with hot winds.
MAY.	106	78	92	98	82	90	21	13	16	W. WSW.	Clear, with hot winds.
JUNE.	107	82	94½	98½	84½	91½	21	8	14	W.SW.	Thermometer in the Sun 114½°. Cloudy, close; slight rain, with thunder and lightning, on the 21st.
JULY.	103	78	90½	95½	85½	90½	17	0	10	W. SW.	Close and sultry; rain for four days without intermission, from 25th to 29th.
AUGUST.	95	78	86½	94½	82	88¼	15	8	12½	S.SW. & S. W.	Thermometer. In the Sun 104°. Cloudy and sultry; thunder and lightning, with rain, on the 30th.
SEPT.	98	75	86½	92½	75½	84	21	7	17	W.SW.	Close and oppressive nights; sultry; flying-showers all round, with thunder and lightning.

N.B. The Instrument suspended in a shady verandah to the N.E.

CHAPTER XXII.

CONCLUSION.

GENERAL VIEW OF CUTCH.

Ancient History of Cutch. — Conflicting Authorities respecting the Route of Alexander the Great over India, — Conquest of the Country by Menander.—Modern History.—British Treaty of 1816, with the Rao Bharmuljee.—Dethronement of the Rao, and Succession of his Son.—Effects of the British Connexion with Cutch.—Aborigines.—Modern Cutchees.—Jharrejah Families.—Jewish Features of the Belluches, and of the Summa Tribes.—Population.—Virtues and Vices of the Cutchee Character.—Habits.—Food.—Love of Opium.—Cutchee Respect for the European Character.—Medical and Surgical Science.—Astronomy.—Eclipses.—The Fine Arts.—Mechanical Skill.—Manufactures and Trade.—Province of Sindh. — Potters. — Money-lenders. — Language of the Boors of Cutch.—Women of Cutch.—Henna.—Children.—Costume of the Rajpoot Tribes.—Dress of the Sindhians.—Feodal Tenures.—Divisions of the Province.—Evils of the Feodal System.—Physical Advantages and Disadvantages of Cutch.

THE ancient history of Cutch is involved in much obscurity, and a great deal of discussion has lately arisen, amongst the learned, as to the exact route pursued by Alexander the Great, through Sindh, and whether, according to the Greek historians, the Macedonian conqueror did or did not march over any portion of Cutch. Dr. Vincent has recorded his belief that he did so march, but other authorities dispute the point.*

To the curious in antiquarian research, the investigation of this knotty question may possess interest; but little profit can arise from it to others. From the constant changes incident to all the branches of the river Indus, any opinion must be offered diffidently: the topic seems suited only for the consideration of those who are personally acquainted with the local features of Cutch and Sindh, and the present state of the river Indus.

Without involving myself or the reader in a labyrinth of unsatisfactory queries and suggestions, I will endeavour merely to sketch the more modern history of Cutch, from the few years which preceded the epoch of its alliance with the British Government.

Until the year 1802, this unhappy country was alike devastated by faction, and harassed by the atrocious profligacy of its rulers, many of whom, without a shadow of legitimate right, supported their lawless oppressions by the aid of mercenary

* For some interesting notices on this subject, I beg to refer my readers to the pages of the Royal Asiatic Society's Journal for November 1834, and to an essay on Vicramaditya and Salivahana, in the 9th volume of the Asiatic Researches, p. 227.

troops, Arabs, Sindhians,* and Meyanna plunderers, the inhabitants of the neighbouring desert.†

After many years of negociation with the British Government, whose interference was earnestly desired by the well-disposed of the community, a treaty was eventually formed in the year 1816, between Rao Bharmuljee, the reigning prince, and the Bombay Government; and a subsidized force of British troops were stationed at Anjar, with the ostensible object of supporting the power of the Rao against his rebellious chiefs. The protection, afforded by the Sindhian Government to the lawless ruffians who then formed the mercenary troops of these chiefs, has frequently

* "As mercenaries, in the pay of the western countries of India, the Sindhian holds the next place to the Arab, a race of men who have, of late years, rendered themselves remarkable for a continued, though unintentional, and brave, though unfortunate opposition to the English troops throughout these territories."—Capt. MacMurdo, *On Sindh.*"

† "The Rajas of Cach'ha boast of their independence, and pretend that, since the beginning of the world, they have never been conquered; and that once they ruled over the whole of Gujrát. They have forgotten the conquest of their country by Menander, which is well attested; for unquestionable vestiges of it remained in the second century; such as temples, altars, fortified camps, and very large wells of masonry, with many coins of Menander and Apollodotus; and these monuments were found as far south as Baroach."—9th volume of the *Asiatic Researches.*

brought us into collision with the Ameers, or rulers of that country, who constantly displayed a spirit of hostility towards us; and so late as 1825, it was found necessary to assemble large bodies of troops in Cutch, to compel these chiefs to a maintenance of their treaty.

The measures taken by Rao Bharmuljee, soon after his alliance with our Government, excited general discontent, and threatened to prove adverse to all quiet and good feeling. He became addicted to gross sensuality, threw all power into the hands of his profligate favourites, and sanctioned every species of tyranny and injustice. To sum up his iniquities, he was proved guilty of the treacherous murder of his cousin, prince Ladoba, under circumstances of unusual atrocity; and in short, his conspiracies, dissipation, and public as well as private profligacy, induced our Government to accept the proffered co-operation of the Jharrejah Bhyaud,* for his dethronement. In 1819, the hill of Bhoojiah was taken by a British army under the command of Sir William Grant Keir, the person of the Rao placed in arrest, and his only son, the young Rao Daisuljee, appointed his successor. During the young prince's minority, his country was governed by a

* Bhyaud means confederated feodal barons, forming a defensive brotherhood.—See Dr. Burnes, *On the History of Cutch.*

regency, in which the name of Colonel Pottinger, the British Resident, was included; but as it has been our policy religiously to abstain from any interference with the internal government of the province, its people retain all those peculiar characteristics which I have endeavoured to describe. Civil faction, however, combined with a most audacious system of piracy on the shores of Cutch, has tended to impoverish the country, and check its commerce. The future steady administration of a wise government may remedy these evils; and for whatever advantages may accrue to this province, the community will be indebted to the temperate measures of the British power. We have now the means of doing much to stimulate industry, to foster the spirit of enquiry, and to develope the resources of the country.

Our connection with Cutch has given us a valuable frontier position; and although it is said, that the sum* we receive annually from the Rao is insufficient to meet the expenses of the subsidy, circumstances may arise, to render our position highly advantageous. Within the range of present prospect, our political horizon presents two views, in which the strength of our frontier position in this province might serve to advance our interests: the one, in which we suppose the anticipated commercial importance of the river

* Two lacs and eighty thousand rupees.

Indus; and the other, arising, possibly, from the perspective anarchy and civil faction which threaten to involve the rich country of the Punjab, on the death of its present ruler, the Maharaja Runjeet Sing.

The people of Cutch were originally a mixture of aboriginal shepherds with a pastoral tribe of Mussulmans imported to it from Sindh.* The latter, in early times, intermarried with the women of the province, and took the title of Jharrejahs as a Rajpoot tribe. The modern Cutchees are a strong, well proportioned, and muscular race of men, rather above the middle size: the higher ranks incline to great corpulence, a beauty much admired and sought after by Asiatics.

The Jharrejah families are distinguished by peculiarly Jewish countenances; and as Captain MacMurdo mentions these as characteristic of some tribes of Sindhians, they probably inherit this singularity of feature from their immediate ancestors.†

The population of Cutch is essentially military,

* Men of the Summa tribe.

† "The Belluches, and many of the Summa tribes, have in a remarkable degree those features commonly called Jewish, and which are strikingly different from those of the other inhabitants. An oval contour of face, aquiline nose, arched eyebrows, and high forehead with expressive eyes, are the characteristic features of the Sindhians above alluded to."—Capt. MacMurdo, *On Sindh.*

and comparatively few of the people follow trade or agriculture: when they do so, it is merely with a view of providing for the urgent necessities of daily life. As a race they are proud, dishonest, indolent, and cunning; sufficiently ingenious as workmen, and by no means indifferent to the possession of money. To explain this seeming inconsistency in the Cutchee character, it will be necessary to remark, that the population consists of two distinct classes: the military class; and those who reside in towns, and follow trade, or other civil occupations. The former devote themselves to luxurious sensuality, whilst the latter are as grasping and avaricious as the majority of their Asiatic brethren. This class is principally Hindu; and, although extremely ingenious as imitative workmen, are neither industrious nor enterprising.

The Cutchees seem to have few of the virtues of Asiatics, and possess many vices essentially their own. Their general ignorance is almost incredible, and their self-sufficiency keeps pace with their ignorance. Even their religious knowledge is confined to their Brahmins and Moolahs, who themselves are incapable of giving any account of their respective creeds; their acquirements extending only to an acquaintance with a few mantras and local legends.

Although in the common affairs of life, these

people are phlegmatic and slothful, on any affair of interest they shout and chatter to each other with astonishing volubility. It is also curious, that the height of angry altercation rarely induces a blow: the altercators bawl and scream at each other with violent gesticulation, but the most provoking personal attack seldom proceeds beyond a push, which is rarely returned. The Hindus regard the Mahomedans with great friendliness, and join in all their festivities.

The Cutchees are simple in their habits of life: their common food is rice, parched grain, or a few vegetables cooked with a little ghee, and eaten with cakes of coarse flour. The better sort of people sometimes indulge in curry and sweetmeats. They profess themselves water-drinkers, but are really addicted to the use of intoxicating liquors, which they distil in all the villages from various vegetable productions. They drink also freely of toddy, which is procured in large quantities from the date and the cocoa-nut palm. Opium is prepared by them, and used both as Kusumba, and in its simple state, in large quantities. It seems less injurious, however, than the Turkish drug, and its effects are less perceptible. The men carry the opium in little boxes, about their persons, and take it at all times.*

* I remember a circumstance which may be worth relating as illustrative of the propensity of people of all ages for this

With this means of refreshment, they are capable of great fatigue, and can journey long and rapidly without food, smoking as they go, and stopping only for a draught of water from the numerous wells.

The Cutchees appear to feel respect for the European character, and are obliging in their intercourse with us. Amongst other notions of our superiority, they believe us to be all astrologers and doctors. In both astrology and medicine, however, they have their adepts ; and great men never hazard a journey without choosing a favourable conjunction of the planets for their departure. There are no fewer than thirty-five Hakeems, or Medicos, in the city of Bhooj ; but, unluckily for their fever patients, not one Sangrado amongst them all. In this strait, the sufferers apply to a carpenter, who has somewhere learnt

drug. We were seated after dinner in a tent near Anjar, when our observation was attracted by approaching travellers, who proved to be itinerant musicians, on their way to the town. One was on foot, and the elder, a grey-headed old gentleman, was mounted on a wretched poney, carrying on his lap his little grandchild, an infant about four months old. We hailed the party, who, turning their wearied poney loose, proceeded to give us a specimen of their art. Whilst the younger traveller unrolled his Vina, the elder, putting his hand to his turban, drew forth his little box of Affeem (opium) and, pinching off a modicum of its contents, gave it to the child, who received it readily, as its accustomed food.

the art of phlebotomy, and operates on them with a phleme. They are equally at a loss for dentists; and the absence of a polished key is remedied by the use of a bent and rusty nail, urged against the offending tooth by an unskilled practitioner.

None of the sciences, either curious or useful, is known even in its simplest elements, to these poor people; yet they show a desire for information, when one wiser than themselves excites their curiosity, which might, ably directed, prove a channel for their general improvement. As it is, they evince that simple result of ignorance, so common in uncivilized minds, the confounding of great and small things, without reference to the superior dignity of the former.* The remains of

* A ludicrous instance of this occurred a short time since, when, some falling stars being observed at noonday, a gentleman sent for the Rao's prime minister, himself an astrologer, to account for the phenomenon. After some consideration, he augured it to foretell civil war, and much bloodshed. Amusingly enough, a few days after this, a skirmish took place at Luckput on the Indus, and one Cutchee was killed. The seer ran triumphant to my friend, delighted at the success of his predictions! *Proh pudor!* The stars falling, to foretell the death of one Cutchee, on the bundee of a petty village!

An eclipse is to these people a source of great astonishment and fear. On the total eclipse of the moon, which took place soon after midnight on the 14th of October, 1837, the whole population of the city of Bhooj were in waiting for the phe-

many specimens of great beauty prove the Cutchees to have once possessed considerable proficiency in some of the arts, especially those of carving, sculpture, and design. I have already remarked on the delicate skill of the goldsmiths, armourers, and embroiderers; and it is calculated to excite surprise that, uninformed as the Cutchees are, and unacquainted, by reason of their local position, as they must be, with the arts practised in other more civilized provinces, they should yet prove such excellent workmen. A view, however, of the general policy of Indian rulers, which has its influence in Cutch as elsewhere, explains this apparent difficulty. It was originally decreed, that only particular castes of men should practise particular arts, and that the exercise of these vocations should descend from generation to

nomenon, which they believe to be caused by an evil spirit, who wars against the moon, and at length conquers, and seizes it in his arms. On the commencement of the eclipse, deep silence attested the anxiety of the multitude; but when the moon's disc became wholly obscured, they raised with one accord the most terrible lamentations, crying out, "*chur do, chur do*," (let go) with voices of loud wailing and entreaty. It produced a startling effect, as we gazed up in the stillness of night, to hear that wild cry in one deep chorus burst forth from a thousand voices, arousing all nature from its hushed and death-like rest. It is customary, on the occurrence of an eclipse, for the Rao to distribute flour, grain, and money to the people.

generation. In obedience to this law, the members of each family are trained to one art, in which they gain unusual expertness, and are enabled to produce articles of unequalled beauty. The amiable and learned historian, Dr. Robertson, remarking on this custom, says, "to it may be ascribed the high degree of perfection conspicuous in many of the Indian manufactures; and though veneration for the practices of their ancestors may check the spirit of invention, yet by adhering to these, they acquire such an expertness and delicacy of hand, that Europeans, with all the advantages of superior science, and the aid of more complete instruments, have never been able to equal the exquisite skill of their workmanship."

The inhabitants of the towns carry on a variety of trades, in addition to the weaving of their woollen and cotton cloths, for the manufacture of which Cutch is famed. For the knowledge of this art they are indebted to the Sindhians, many of whom conduct this trade at Mandavie. The cloths are usually woven in a small chequered pattern, with bright and variously coloured borders. This circumstance is perhaps curious, the peculiar manufacture being of considerable antiquity, in the neighbouring province of Sindh, and the original Cutch manufacturers being men of T'hatta, which modern writers have reasonably identified with the Pátála* of the Greeks, a city in all ages celebrated for the superior manufacture of its looms. To T'hatta† Sir William Jones probably referred, when, speaking of the chief articles of Indian trade, he says, "fine linen is conjectured, with some probability, to have been called by the ancients Sindou, from the name of the river Indus, or Sindhus, near which it was wrought in the highest perfection." The present manufacture of Cutch is a coarse and inferior fabric, but much prized in the neighbouring provinces, and exported in large quantities from Mandavie, in return for various articles of merchandise received from Zanzibar and the ports of the Red Sea.‡

* According to Dr. Robertson, the first place in India, to which ships from Egypt, while they followed the ancient course of navigation, were accustomed to trade, was Patala, on the river Indus. They imported to it, woollen cloth of a slight fabric, *linen in chequer work*, precious stones, &c.

† The word T'hatta signifies closely populated. A Persian writer states the country to have been originally peopled from Yúman, which is supposed to be Greek. T'hatta, now in a low state of impoverishment, was not only celebrated as the great emporium of Indian and Arabian commerce, but also for its learned and able men.

‡ It is to be regretted, that this useful art is not improved in Cutch, as the province possesses great capabilities. The Cutch sheep produce good wool; but the people are quite ignorant of the best means of procuring and dressing it. The country appears so congenial to these animals, that I should

The potters are, as may be inferred from the fragile nature of their wares, a busy race; and the shroffs, or money-lenders, are a remarkable caste, labouring only to keep up the "rate of usance," and as greedy in the receipt of their interest as any Shylock on the Rialto. They are ever lean, rent, and hungered; and were each worth an argosy, they would still be the most filthy and wretched looking of the community.

The common language of the boors of Cutch is a rude and barbarous *patois;* but the Jharrejahs, who brought the Sindh language into the country, continue to speak it, with pure Hindustanee, as the language of the court.* The shepherd aborigines of Cutch retain the Guzzerati, which is the only written tongue used in the province.

think much advantage might accrue to any capitalist who would introduce the merino, or any superior kind, at the same time instructing the natives in preparing the wool according to the system pursued so successfully in New South Wales. By this means, and by the application of machinery, the art once so highly prized might be revived, and the produce become an article of considerable commerce, affording a commensurate return to the speculatist.

* Captain McMurdo says, that he believes the Sindhi to be a branch of the Sanskreet stock, which has supplied India with languages; and he advances this opinion, from their affinity, the radicals of many of the words being alike, and the language itself containing a greater number of Sanskreet words than the Guzzerati, which is a pure Hindu dialect.

The women of Cutch are in figure unusually slight, and possess countenances rather interesting than beautiful. The women of Mandavie form an exception, many of them being strikingly handsome. Their general manners are pleasing and gentle; and, from the usual grace of their actions, I should infer, that a Cutchee woman, under the influence of social circumstances more congenial to the development of female character, might become a very fascinating ornament of society. Unhappily, however, they are now condemned to every description of menial drudgery; and, contemned as they are by their indolent masters, it is almost a matter of surprise that the impulse afforded by mere female vanity should prove sufficiently strong to induce them to braid their hair, and ornament their persons with the care which is every where apparent. Were it possible for a Hindu woman once to feel herself an object of regard to the other sex — could she once learn to estimate her own worth, in creation's scale — could her full dark eye beam with intelligence, and her lips speak the language of feeling, she would yield to few in attractiveness and grace, and to none, perhaps, in the native gentleness of her character, and the simple elegance of her general deportment. Separated, however, as these women are from such advantages of civilized opinion, the taste of the observer is pained to see so much artless grace enslaved by ignorance, and so much real beauty condemned to the most filthy and disgusting labours. Notwithstanding the delicacy of her appearance, a Cutchee woman is capable of great exertion, and she pursues the fatiguing routine of daily duty without a murmur of discontent. At early dawn she grinds the corn for family consumption, collects the materials for firing, cleans the cooking utensils, and sweeps out the dwelling. Then, with probably a tier of three water-vessels on her head, an infant seated on one hip, which she supports with her arm passed round its body, and an elder child clinging to her skirts, she walks to the nearest well, or tank, returns with the water, cooks the family meal, and sits down to her spinning-wheel. After this, she again goes to the tank to wash herself and her clothes. This, indeed, constitutes her sole amusement. Divested of her upper clothing, she sits in the water laughing and chatting to her neighbours, or trolling some simple ditty, as, with garments neatly tucked around her, she beats her linen against a stone, or holds aloft her gaily coloured saree, to dry and warm in the sunny breeze.

The Hindu and Mahomedan women marry early, until which event they are not permitted to wear either nose-rings, or henna, the favourite adornment of an Asiatic beauty.* As widows, also, they are forbidden the use of ornaments. The Hindu women of the province wear the Mandavie dress already described; but the Mahomedan women continue the ungraceful dress of the trowsers and frock, common to the female descendants of the founder of the faith.

The Cutchee children are unusually pretty, good-tempered, and interesting: they seldom encumber themselves with dress until about seven years of age, when the little girls at once adopt the full petticoat, saree, anklets, bangles, and the whole adornment of womanhood. Ill adapted as this costume would be to the habits of English children, the subdued manners of the Hindus render it suitable to these little damsels, who arrange the folds of their sarees, to shade their

* Henna is produced from a pretty shrub, called in India Mendee, and by English botanists Lawsonia. The shrub has small leaves, and a very sweet-scented blossom, in some degree resembling the clematis. Henna is prepared by bruising the leaves, and moistening them with water and a little lime-juice. They are then applied to the nails, tips of the fingers, and palms of the hands, which in a short time become dyed of a dark orange colour. The stain remains on the skin for many days, and is not affected by either water or vegetable acids. I had always imagined that Henna produced a rosy tint on the skin, and perhaps it may do so, if procured from a finer description of Mendee, or if differently prepared.

sunny cheeks and sparkling eyes, with all the grace of a more advanced age. The boys, whilst very young, wear their hair platted, and hanging down the back; but as lads, they adopt the Doputta, a huge turban, and the Brahminical thread.*

The dress worn by the poorer sort of people in Cutch, is a simple white cotton body cloth,† made to fit the person, and descending to the knees. It is bound round the waist with a strip of coloured linen, which serves as a turban, or a cummerbund, as occasion may require.

The Rajpoot tribes wear the Ankrika with remarkably long and loose sleeves, confined round the waist with the Doputta. A dark coloured cloth which descends to the knees; a pair of loose linen trowsers confined with a single button at the ankle; an immense turban, and a great variety of embroidered pouches, complete this very picturesque costume.

The Sindhians, as they are seen at Mandavie, wear loose trowsers of blue cotton under a frock of the same colour, with a cummerbund and turban of T'hatta manufacture, folded round a conical and thickly quilted cap.

The government, and the system of landed

* Called the Junnoee; a sacred cord, peculiar to the order of Brahmins, and adopted by them at a very early age.

† Called an Ankrika.

proprietorship in Cutch, are remarkable, and present a surprising resemblance to the feodal baronies of England.

The province is portioned into five great divisions, and the lands which compose them are held by chiefs on feodal tenure.

The Rao of Cutch is himself a Rajpoot, and the Lord Paramount of a Bhyaud of Jharrejahs. These chiefs enjoy grants of land, for which they pay no revenue, but, in return, owe military service to the Rao.

The investiture of a chief takes place at the Durbar, where the Rao presents him with a killat, or dress of honour, a trifling present of jewels, and other marks of his favour. The lands so entrusted are hereditary, but may be forfeited by misconduct, and are liable to confiscation on breach of contract.

The second division of land is held by the Rajpoot Wagelas, on a feodal tenure called Jumma Bundee.* These chiefs are rated according to their number of ploughs, and again owe military service to their immediate lords, the Jharrejah chiefs.

The third link in the feodal chain is the tenure of the Grasias, minor tenants, who, like the Wagelas, farm villages, and pay a slight tax.

The fourth division of land consists of villages

* Jumma Bundee, literally meaning, "to collect together."

and lands, granted to peers, hutteets, and other holy men; as also for the benefit of religious and charitable institutions. From these the Rao derives no revenue.

From the remaining lands, the Rao receives a share of their produce in kind. These are called Bhog, which signifies to enjoy.

The original object of these grants must have been to secure the service of the federal chiefs, their followers, and retainers, in circumstances of common danger to the country from foreign powers. But though all the chiefs, retainers, and vassals, so invested with feodal rights, are either directly or indirectly bound to give service to the Rao as their Lord Paramount, the obligation has been frequently evaded; and the system, in early times, served only to foster mutiny, and give rise to private dissension; the inferior chiefs always supporting the power of their immediate lords, even against that of their prince.

Since the Hindu connexion with the British government, any possible advantage to be gained by the Rao from the attachment of his federal adherents has ceased, and the lands so apportioned conduce only to general impoverishment.

The evils of this system are numerous and important. Not only has it reduced the revenues of the Rao, who has little more than is sufficient to meet the expenses of the subsidy, but as his principal resources are now derived from the large towns of Anjar, Mandavie, Bhooj, Jakow, and Luckput, three of which are sea-ports burthened by heavy transit duties, it compels him to farm these revenues. This, whilst it produces a certain return to the royal treasury, must, as a system, ever be the cause of a greater or less degree of oppression to the subject.

Such are the social evils, which, having outlived the times that gave them birth, continue to oppose the interests and objects of commercial improvement. For many years this province has been alternately exposed to the ferocious despotism of its rulers, and the lawless rapacity of such bandit mercenaries as were bribed to become the auxiliaries of its rebellious chiefs. The barrenness of the soil, and the scantiness of its population, are at once explained by such a political aspect; and the mingled ignorance, indolence, and social immorality of its people, are ascribable to the same influences.

Subject to arbitrary seizures of their property, the agricultural part of the population became indolent, and cunning, in proportion to the urgent necessities of self-interest; whilst the feodal education of the military tribes fostered in them all the pride and ferocity of the rudest barbarism.

A little reflection will convince every liberal reader, that a people who, under so many disadvantages, have yet displayed so much ingenuity in works of art—whose sea-ports possess so many advantages for commerce—and whose country contains so many natural resources, must be eminently fitted to receive improvement under a state of greater political civilization. With the interest which a long residence amongst them has induced me to feel for a people, whose amiable qualities are all their own, and whose vices are the result of uncongenial circumstances, happy indeed shall I be, if the rapid glance I have endeavoured to give of their present condition should excite an interest for the natives of Cutch, that might eventually acquire for them those blessings of intelligence, which can be enjoyed only through the means of commercial, agricultural, and mental culture.

> "Ingenious arts, where they an entrance find,
> Soften the manners, and subdue the mind."

THE END.

THE LIBRARY OF ROMANCE:

A HIGHLY INTERESTING SERIES OF 15 VOLS.

COMPRISING

ORIGINAL TALES, NOVELS, AND ROMANCES,

BY THE MOST DISTINGUISHED WRITERS OF THE DAY.

PRICE ONLY SIX SHILLINGS PER VOLUME;

EACH VOLUME COMPLETE IN ITSELF,

AND EQUAL IN EXTENT TO THREE VOLUMES OF THE MODERN NOVELS.

Fifteen volumes of this work — allowed to be the boldest literary speculation to which the enterprize of the age has given birth — are now published; the reception they have met with — the praises lavished upon the work, and upon the romances individually, by the British press, have been warm and universal; each volume has been reprinted in America; they have almost all been translated into German, many into French; and some have been reprinted at Paris, in the original language, for the accommodation of the English abroad. The names of BANIM, FRASER, GALT, the late ANDREW PICKEN, VICTOR HUGO, the Author of "Tales of a Physician;" the Author of "Wild Sports of the West," LEITCH RITCHIE, &c., grace the list of Authors, and prove that the word of promise has been kept to the fullest extent.

The following is a Catalogue of the Series.

I. THE GHOST HUNTER AND HIS FAMILY. A Tale from the powerful pen of BANIM. Exhibiting a Picture of Irish Manners; supposed to be the most striking, as well as the most beautiful of the works of this well-known master.

II. SCHINDERHANNES, THE ROBBER OF THE RHINE. A Romantic Sketch, drawn up from Historical and Legal Documents of the celebrated Banditti System of Germany. By the Editor, LEITCH RITCHIE.

III. WALTHAM. A Domestic Narrative. By the late ANDREW PICKEN. Anatomizing some of the most strange and mystic Sympathies of our Nature, in illustration of the Doctrine of Fatalism.

IV. THE STOLEN CHILD; A TALE OF THE TOWN. Detailing, in the minute and original manner of its Author, GALT, one of the most remarkable histories of evidence ever penned—in reference, it is understood, to a very important event in an illustrious family.

V. THE BONDMAN. An Historical Narrative of the Times of Wat Tyler. The production of MRS. O'NEILL. The Work is filled with historical and legal knowledge, and presents a romantic picture, not less accurate than extraordinary, of one of the most singular epochs of our history.

VI. THE SLAVE KING. A skilful and elegant adaptation of the BUG JARGAL of VICTOR HUGO. Containing a romantic and historical description of the Rebellion of the Blacks of Saint Domingo. By ELIZABETH MARGARET RITCHIE. Illustrated with Notes, contributed by a recent Traveller.

VII. THE KHAN'S TALE. A TALE OF THE CARAVANSERAI. By JAMES BAILLIE FRASER. Exhibiting a picture of Persian manners of the same kind as that which at once startled and delighted the public in his "Kuzzilbash."

VIII. WALDEMAR; OR, THE SACK OF MAGDEBURG. A TALE OF THE THIRTY YEARS' WAR. In which the skilful Author of "Tales of a Physician," has chosen for the exercise of his vivid pencil the most romantic period in Modern History.

IX. THE DARK LADY OF DOONA. By the Author of "Wild Sports of the West." An Irish Romance of the time of Elizabeth, so singular and so powerful, that the *Athenæum* fairly confesses that "criticism would be as idle as reading the riot-act at Donybrook fair—not a soul would pay it the least attention."

X. THE BARONET; OR, L'AMANT MALGREBLIN. A picture of living Manners in the present Fashionable World. By Miss J. CORNER.

XI. THE SEA-WOLF. A Romance of "The Free Traders." A Naval Narrative, of wild and exciting interest, founded on facts, and presenting many points of relation with the celebrated fictions of Cooper.

XII. THE JESUIT. A powerful and striking illustration of the principles and practices of that celebrated Society, from which it takes its name—including transactions springing out of the disastrous attempt of the Pretender on the Throne of Great Britain.

XIII. THE SIEGE OF VIENNA, An Historical Narrative. By MADAME PICHLER; containing an account of one of the most splendid and picturesque events of the seventeenth century, in which the Poles under Sobieski, took so prominent a part.

XIV. THE ENTHUSIAST; OR, TRAITS AND CHARACTERISTICS OF THE GERMAN COURT. An adaptation of one of the Romances of SPINDLER. An admirably wrought and striking Narrative, full of faith, grace, and affection, and in every way worthy of its high reputation, reminding us, in its *denouement*, of the Vicar of Wakefield.

XV. ERNESTO; OR, THE HISTORY OF A MIND. A Philosophical Romance. By WILLIAM SMITH, Esq. Author of "Guidone."

"The Library of Romance is, unquestionably, one of the cheapest, the best, and most tastefully got up works of the kind to which modern bibliopolic spirit and enterprise have given birth. It will indeed be a standard work, and will be sought after and read with avidity when its contemporary works of fiction are utterly forgotten."—*Observer*.

Works on Emigration.

Second Edition in 2 vols. 8vo. price 28s. illustrated with a large Map of Australia, by Arrowsmith; Charts, Fossils, Landscapes, and beautifully coloured Plates of Birds, &c.

RECENT DISCOVERIES IN AUSTRALIA.

A NARRATIVE OF TWO

Expeditions into the Interior of Australia,

UNDERTAKEN BY CAPTAIN CHARLES STURT, OF THE 39TH REGIMENT,

By order of the Colonial Government,

To ascertain the nature of the Country to the west and north-west of the Colony of New South Wales.

"We heartily recommend these volumes to public notice. They are full of interest; well and modestly written, carefully illustrated, and, on the whole, make us better acquainted with the interior of Australia and its native tribes than any other work we have hitherto met with."—*Athenæum.*

In one vol. demy 8vo. price 14s. boards.

THE PRESENT STATE OF AUSTRALIA,

A DESCRIPTION OF THE COUNTRY,

ITS ADVANTAGES AND PROSPECTS WITH REFERENCE TO EMIGRATION;

And a particular Account of the Manners, Customs, and Condition of its Aboriginal Inhabitants.

BY ROBERT DAWSON, ESQ.

Late Chief Agent of the Australian Agricultural Company.

"The work before us is an important work on a very important question. The Author's advice to emigrants ought to be read by every one contemplating a trip to a remote colony, from whence they may not have the power easily to retreat. The most valuable portion of Mr. Dawson's volume is unquestionably the mass of practical information it affords to all persons contemplating emigration."—*New Monthly Magazine.*

Second Edition in one vol. demy 8vo. illustrated with a Map of Australia, and Five coloured Plates, price 16s. boards.

THE FRIEND OF AUSTRALIA,

CONTAINING

Observations on the immense Benefits of Emigration,

OF FORMING NEW SETTLEMENTS,

And the importance of elucidating the Geography of Australia;

Treating at length of its mysterious Interior,

With Plans for Exploring and Surveying the same with safety;

Plans and Methods of forming Tanks and Reservoirs as practised in India,

Recommended, and Illustrated with Wood-Cuts, &c.

BY AN OFFICER IN THE E. I. COMPANY'S SERVICE.

"This work contains much valuable information respecting the social, moral, and physical condition of Australia. The Author's suggestions for Colonization, &c. are for the most part worthy the attention of the Legislature."—*Observer.*

In two vols. small 8vo. with Map, price 21s. boards.

AN HISTORICAL AND STATISTICAL ACCOUNT OF

NEW SOUTH WALES;

BOTH AS A PENAL SETTLEMENT, AND AS A BRITISH COLONY.

BY JOHN DUNMORE LANG, D.D.

Senior Minister of the Scots Church, and Principal of the Australian College, Sydney.

Second Edition, bringing down the History of the Colony to the end of 1836.

Just published, price Sixpence,

OBSERVATIONS ON THE ADVANTAGES OF EMIGRATION TO NEW SOUTH WALES,

FOR THE INFORMATION OF THE LABOURING CLASSES IN THE UNITED KINGDOM;

Comprising valuable Extracts from the Minutes of Evidence taken before a Committee of the Council at Sydney;

Also the Report of the Chief Justice to his Excellency;
With other authentic and useful information just received from the Colony.

THE EMIGRANT AND TRAVELLER'S GUIDE, TO AND THROUGH CANADA,

BY WAY OF THE RIVER ST. LAWRENCE, AS WELL AS BY WAY OF THE UNITED STATES:

With some friendly advice on Embarkation:
The detailed Cost of Travelling on each Route, and other useful information to Settlers.

BY JOHN MURRAY. Price 1*s.* 6*d.*

"This will be found a useful unpretending little volume. Mr. Murray has himself seen the country he describes, and speaks of expenses, routes, wages, distances, &c., from actual experience. To the emigrant to Canada the book is invaluable; for, from his embarkation to the time of settling, it never leaves him. It shows the difference of money in England and America; the best and most economical modes of travelling; the productions of the country; and describes with clearness the remarkable places through which the traveller passes."—*True Sun.*

In two vols. 8vo. price £1 8s. bds.

THE HISTORY OF THE Twelve Great Livery Companies of London,

PRINCIPALLY COLLECTED FROM THEIR GRANTS AND RECORDS,

WITH NOTES AND ILLUSTRATIONS,

AN HISTORICAL INTRODUCTION, AND COPIOUS ACCOUNTS OF EACH COMPANY AND OF THEIR ESTATES AND CHARITIES,

WITH

ATTESTED COPIES AND TRANSLATIONS OF ALL THE COMPANIES' CHARTERS FROM THEIR FOUNDATION TO THE PRESENT TIME.

BY WILLIAM HERBERT,
Librarian to the Corporation of London.

The Histories of the various Companies may be had separately at the following prices in cloth boards.

CLOTHWORKERS, 4*s.*	GROCERS, 7*s.*	MERCHANT TAILORS, 8*s.*
DRAPERS, 8*s.*	HABERDASHERS, 4*s.*	SALTERS, 4*s.*
FISHMONGERS, 8*s.*	IRONMONGERS, 6*s.*	SKINNERS, 7*s.*
GOLDSMITHS, 10*s.*	MERCERS, 7*s.*	VINTNERS, 4*s.*

In demy 8vo. with a Map and Plates, price 14s.

SIX YEARS IN BISCAY:

COMPRISING

A Personal Narrative of the Sieges of Bilbao,

IN JUNE 1835, AND OCTOBER TO DECEMBER 1836;

AND OF THE PRINCIPAL EVENTS WHICH OCCURRED IN THAT CITY AND THE BASQUE PROVINCES, DURING THE YEARS 1830 TO 1837.

BY JOHN FRANCIS BACON.

"This is an able work, and it appears opportunely, for it makes the public well acquainted with what is called the Spanish Question."—*Sunday Review.*

"This work is written by a gentleman who resided for six years in the heart of the insurgent districts, the account given is frank and clear, and drawn entirely from personal observation. It gives much information of an available kind to the general reader, that is not to be found in any of the numerous publications that have been generated by the unnatural war in Spain."—*Atlas.*

"This volume will well repay the perusal of any person interested in the present contest in Spain, and wishing to arrive at the truth respecting it. The work is altogether one of the best we have met with on the subject of the present Spanish war of succession."—*Naval and Military Gazette.*

"To all who desire to receive further information as to the cause, the present state, and the probable result of the civil war in Spain, we can recommend this work. The writer resided long in the country—in Bilbao—the very centre of operations; he was both observing and inquiring, and has collected together a vast many facts, throwing light on the state of the Basque Provinces before the war, on the causes of the protracted struggle, the endless failures of the Queen's Generals, &c."—*Athenæum.*

In demy 8vo. price 14s. boards, with a Portrait and other Plates.

THE LIFE OF

ADMIRAL VISCOUNT EXMOUTH,

DRAWN UP FROM OFFICIAL AND OTHER AUTHENTIC DOCUMENTS SUPPLIED BY HIS FAMILY AND FRIENDS.

BY EDWARD OSLER, ESQ.

This Memoir has been undertaken with the sanction of Lord Exmouth's elder and only surviving Brother, whose recollections, and a correspondence which extends over more than fifty years, in which Lord Exmouth communicates his views and motives without reserve, have supplied the chief materials for a personal history.

"Here is a valuable addition to our Naval Biography: a book not to be read by Englishmen without pride of heart. The name of Exmouth occupies an honourable place beside those of Nelson and Collingwood: his services were hardly less numerous or brilliant than theirs."—*Athenæum.*

"This is a valuable memoir of an officer, whom this country will ever acknowledge as one of its most brilliant heroes. We have had to notice many valuable historical memoirs, but on no occasion have we had more pleasure than in the examination of the one before us: the life of a man whose gallantry and talents won for him the respect and esteem of every officer in the British Navy."—*Naval and Military Gazette.*

"This is the most admirably written and interesting naval memoir which has appeared since THE LIFE OF NELSON. It is a book which no blue-jacket ought to be without. It is rarely, indeed, that we have met with a naval memoir from the pen of a landsman, which realizes so completely our notions of the qualifications requisite in this class of writing, as the volume before us. Its style is simple, energetic, and often eloquent and impressive."—*United Service Gazette.*

"A book full of interesting anecdotes of a noble specimen of English character."—*Times.*

"This volume ought to rank among the first biographical works we possess of our great naval commanders."—*Gentleman's Magazine.*

In foolscap 8vo. beautifully illustrated, price 7s. in fancy cloth.

THE PROGRESS OF CREATION

CONSIDERED

With Reference to the Present Condition of the Earth.

An interesting and useful Work for Young People.

BY MARY ROBERTS, Author of "Annals of My Village," &c. &c.

"This volume forms a profitable addition to that important class of works which now abound in our language, whose aim is to improve the heart through the understanding, by making the discoveries of science subservient to the great interest of religion. We particularly recommend this work as eminently calculated to exalt the mind and purify the heart."—*Scots Times.*

Splendid Illustrations to Byron's Works.

Just completed in Twelve Monthly Parts, price 2s. 6d. each.

COMPRISING, FOR THE FIRST TIME, HISTORICAL AND DESCRIPTIVE LETTER-PRESS, A NEW AND EXTENDED SERIES OF

THE BYRON GALLERY.

A series of Historical Embellishments to illustrate the Poetical Works of Lord Byron; beautifully engraved from Drawings and Paintings by the most celebrated Artists, and adapted by their size and excellence, to bind up with, and embellish every edition published in England of LORD BYRON'S WORKS, and also the various sizes and editions published in France, Germany, and America; ample directions being given for placing them in the respective editions.

A LIMITED NUMBER OF PROOFS HAVE BEEN TAKEN ON ROYAL QUARTO.

Price, on plain paper 4s. India 5s. India before the Letters, 7s.

Sets of the Plates, without the letter-press, may be procured for binding up with the various Editions of

LORD BYRON'S WORKS.

COPIES MAY ALSO BE HAD ELEGANTLY BOUND IN MOROCCO, FORMING A SPLENDID ORNAMENT FOR THE DRAWING-ROOM TABLE.

"Adequately to describe the delicate beauty of these splendid Plates, does not appear to lie within the power of language. There is not an admirer of the works of the departed Noble Poet, who can feel satisfied that he has a perfect edition of them, unless the 'Byron Gallery,' be attached to it. There is no instance in which excellence in poetry and the arts are so admirably combined."—*Imperial Magazine.*

"The most enthusiastic admirer of Byron must now be completely gratified: this Series of Historical Embellishments, will supply a splendid memorial of the noble and immortal Bard. 'The Byron Gallery' was really wanted to make the charm complete; and is executed in a manner worthy of the 'glorious imaginings' which it is the professed object of the work to set before us. The execution of the Engravings is quite masterly."—*Scotsman.*

Just completed, in Ten Monthly Numbers, price 2s. 6d. each.

STANFIELD'S COAST SCENERY.

COMPRISING

A Series of the most Picturesque Views in the British Channel.

FROM ORIGINAL DRAWINGS TAKEN EXPRESSLY FOR THIS PUBLICATION.

BY CLARKSON STANFIELD, ESQ. R.A.

The work is published in super-royal, 8vo., each Part containing Four beautifully finished Line Engravings, by the most eminent Artists, accompanied by highly interesting typographical descriptions, forming altogether one of the most splendid works of the kind which has ever appeared.

A very limited number of proofs have been taken from these splendid Engravings, on Colombier—Imperial and Royal 4to.

*** Copies of "*this truly British and National Work,*" may now be had done up in appropriate and elegant morocco binding, price 32s. 6d. forming an attractive and unique ornament for the Library or Drawing Room Table.

"It seems almost a sin against patriotism, as well as good taste, not to possess oneself of a work so peculiarly National, and so exceedingly beautiful."—*Metropolitan.*

"Amidst the unnumbered embellishments for the Drawing-room Table, or the Portfolio, which are now brought within the reach of every one, the difficulty is to know what is the most worthy of our choice. As directors, though in humble sphere, of the public taste, we would wish as opportunity offers, to point out those works of art which deserve peculiarly the public patronage. With this feeling we introduce the work now before us, assured that the admirers of coast scenery,—and who in the south of Hampshire is not one? will be gratified with these exquisite engravings of subjects taken from both sides of the British Channel."
Hampshire Independent.

In foolscap 8vo. price 7s. handsomely bound in cloth.

THE

TRAVELS OF MINNA AND GODFREY

IN MANY LANDS.

FROM THE JOURNALS OF THE AUTHOR.

HOLLAND.

BEAUTIFULLY ILLUSTRATED FROM THE OLD DUTCH MASTERS.

"Much agreeable and useful information is conveyed in this excellent little work. A high moral is inculcated throughout. Though directed to the young, it is worthy the perusal of adults."—*Sunday Times.*

"A charming little volume; in which the company of two observant children and their remarks, lead to many statements in the course of travels in Holland, which cannot fail to be read with pleasure and instruction, not only by the young, but the more mature. The work has very numerous and clever illustrations, and is well deserving of adoption into all family circles."—*Literary Gazette.*

"This is truly a delightful and useful little book, abounding in information on a country that is less frequently visited and talked of than it deserves.— It is written for young people, but many who have arrived at the age of manhood may read it with advantage."—*Metropolitan.*

"This clever little book belongs, we rather think, to quite a new class. It is neither an original essay prepared from reading or reflection, nor a compilation of facts, adapted to the childish capacity; but the bona fide narrative of a tour, comprehending that species of information which a child is capable of acquiring and enjoying."—*Commentator.*

THE CELEBRATED BLIND TRAVELLER.

In four vols. demy 8vo. illustrated by several highly finished Lithographic Views, and a Portrait of the Author, price 14s. each, (sold separately).

A VOYAGE ROUND THE WORLD;

INCLUDING

Travels in Africa, Asia, Australasia, America, &c. &c.

BY LIEUT. JAMES HOLMAN, R.N. F.R.S.

"This episode in the record of Travels is almost incredible."—*Atlas.*

"This publication is one of the literary wonders of the age."—*Spectator.*

"For this work we cannot but anticipate a circulation as wide, we were going to say, as the Author's Travels."—*Literary Gazette.*

"We have seldom met with any work so replete with interesting information."—*Observer.*

"Lieutenant Holman's work is one of the most extraordinary that has ever appeared in any age or country."—*True Sun.*

In two vols. demy 8vo. price 28s.

A HISTORY OF CHINA,

Ancient and Modern:

COMPRISING

A RETROSPECT OF THE FOREIGN INTERCOURSE AND TRADE WITH CHINA.

ILLUSTRATED BY A NEW AND CORRECTED MAP OF THE EMPIRE.

BY THE REV. CHARLES GUTZLAFF,

NOW AND FOR MANY YEARS PAST, RESIDENT IN THAT COUNTRY.

"Mr. Charles Gutzlaff, a native of Prussia, was employed as a Missionary in the East, we believe, by the Netherlands Society, and to his astonishing skill in acquiring the Dialects of the Chinese Countries, his bold and adventurous character, commerce and statistical science, as well as Christianity, are already indebted. ...... After residing in Siam for some months, preaching, teaching, and acquiring languages, he proceeded to China in a native Junk, and by this mode of travelling, he of course acquired an insight into the character of the lower classes of Chinese. .... In two subsequent voyages he coasted a large part of Western China, during which he was repeatedly charged by the Chinese Mandarins with being a native, so accurate was his knowledge of their language and manners. China, therefore, seems to be a theatre peculiarly fitted for a person of Mr. Gutzlaff's qualifications and temperament."—*Times.*

English	Turkish	Pronunciation
sunflower	*ay çiçe**ği***	uy chicheghi
tree trunk	*ağaç göv**desi***	ughuch ge͡uvdesi
tulip	*lâle*	la͡ale
turnip	*şalgam*	shulgum
violet	*menekşe*	menekshe
wallflower	*şebboy*	shebba͡uy
walnut	*ceviz*	jeviz
willow tree	*söğüt ağacı*	se͡ughe͡wt ughuji(*r*)

Colours

(Renk**ler**)

English	Turkish	Pronunciation
Auburn	*kumral*	ko͡omrul
black	*siyah*	siyuh
black (horse)	*yağız*	yughi(*r*)z
black (or brown) eyed	*kara göz**lü***	kuru ge͡uzle͡w
black-haired	*siyah saç**lı***	siyuh suchli(*r*)
blue	*mavi*	muvi
— (saxe)	*çini mavi**si***	chini muvisi
— (royal)	*açı**k** lacivert*	uchi(*r*)k lujivert
— (navy)	*lacivert*	lujivert
— (sky)	*açı**k** mavi*	uchi(*r*)k muvi
blue-eyed	*mavi göz**lü***	muvi ge͡uzle͡w
bluish-grey-eyed	*çakır göz**lü***	chuki(*r*)r ge͡uzle͡w
brown (coffee colour)	*kahve rengi*	kuhve rengi
— (dark) ,, ,,	*koyu kahve rengi*	ka͡uyo͡o kuhve rengi
brown (horse)	*doru*	da͡uro͡o
chestnut	*kestane rengi*	kestune rengi
cream	*krem*	krem
crimson	*koyu kırmızı*	ka͡uyo͡o ki(*r*)rmi(*r*)zi(*r*)
dark (colour)	*koyu (renk)*	ka͡uyo͡o
dark (complexioned)	*esmer (beniz)*	esmer
faded (colour)	*sol**gun** (renk)*	sa͡ulgo͡on
fair-haired (blonde)	*lepiska saç**lı***	lepisku suchli(*r*)
flame	*ateş rengi*	utesh rengi
green	*yeşil*	yeshil

English	Turkish	Pronunciation
green (bottle)	*nefti*	nefti
— (leaf)	*yaprak yeşili*	yupruk yeshili
grey	*kül rengi*	kew͡l rengi
— (squirrel)	*sincâbî*	sinja͡abe͡e
hazel-eyed	*ela gözlü*	elu ge͡uzle͡w
light (colour)	*açık*	uchi(*r*)k
light (complexioned)	*buğday benizli*	bo͡oghduy benizli
mauve	*eflatun*	efluto͡on
orange	*turuncu*	to͡oro͡onjo͡o
pale (complexioned)	*solgun benizli*	sa͡ulgo͡on benizli
pink	*penbe*	penbe
purple	*mor*	ma͡ur
red	*kırmızı*	ki(*r*)rmi(*r*)zi(*r*)
rust colour	*pas rengi*	pus rengi
scarlet	*al*	ul
silver	*gümüşî*	ge͡wme͡wshe͡e
violet	*menekşe*	menekshe
white	*beyaz, ak*	beyuz, uk
white-haired	*ak saçlı*	uk suchli(*r*)
yellow	*sarı*	suri(*r*)
— (canary)	*kanarya sarısı*	kunuryu suri(*r*)si(*r*)

Things Seen in Town or Country

(Şehir ve sayfiye**de** göz**e** çarp**an** şey**ler**)

English	Turkish	Pronunciation
Bank (money)	*banka (para)*	bunku (puru)
— (of river)	*nehir kenarı*	nehir kenuri(*r*)
barley	*arpa*	urpu
barn	*ambar*	umbur
beehive	*arı kovanı*	ari(*r*) ka͡uvuni(*r*)
bridge	*köprü*	ke͡upre͡w
building	*binâ*	bina͡a
bush	*çalı*	chuli(*r*)
castle	*kal'e, hisar*	kul'e, hisur
cattle	*davar*	duvur
cow, ox	*inek, öküz*	inek, e͡uke͡wz
club (social)	*kulüp*	ko͡ole͡wp
corn	*hububat, zahire, tahıl*	ho͡obo͡obut, zuhire tuhi(*r*)l